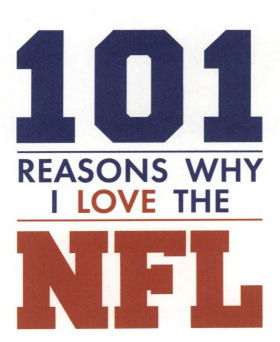

© Danann Publishing Limited 2024

First published in the UK by Sona Books, an imprint of Danann Media Publishing Limited

The right of Scott Reeves to be identified as Author of this Work has been asserted by him in accordance with the Copyright, Designs and Patents Act 1988

WARNING: For private domestic use only, any unauthorised copying, hiring, lending or public performance of this book is illegal.

CAT NO. SONO613

Cover and book design: Darren Grice & Kevin Gardner

Editor: Martin Corteel

Proof reader: Cameron Thurlow

All rights reserved. No part of this title may be reproduced or transmitted in any material form (including photocopying or storing it in any medium by electronic means and whether or not transiently or incidentally to some other use of this publication) without the written permission of the copyright owner, except in accordance with the provisions of the Copyright, Designsand Patents Act 1988. Applications for the copyright owner's written permission should be addressed to the publisher.

Printed in EU

ISBN: 978-1-915343-79-6

This is an independent publication and it is unofficial and unauthorised and as such has no connection with the National Football League (NFL) or any other organisation connected in any way whatsoever with the NFL featured in the book.

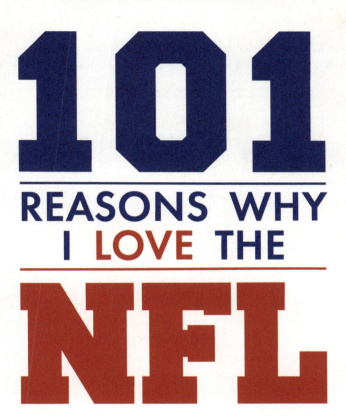

INTRODUCTION

When the reigning champion Kansas City Chiefs took on the San Francisco 49ers at Super Bowl LVIII on 11 February 2024, the game was a record-breaker. An average of 123.4 million people watched the game in the United States: most tuned in to the CBS broadcast with Jim Nantz and Tomy Romo in the commentary box; streamers caught it on Paramount+; while young viewers had their own broadcast on Nickelodeon. Only the Apollo 11 moon landing captured the attention of more American viewers – and there were millions more watching around the world. Sports fans were enthralled by the stories involved. Patrick Mahomes continued his quest to be named the greatest player of all time. Brock Purdy aimed to become Super Bowl champion, barely a year after being the last pick in the NFL Draft. Music sensation Taylor Swift jetted in straight from a concert in Japan to support her new boyfriend, Kansas City's **Travis Kelce**.

Super Bowl LVIII didn't disappoint the mammoth TV audience. After trailing 10-3 at half-time, the Chiefs stormed back into contention. 49ers kicker Jake Moody had an extra point blocked in the fourth quarter before his Kansas City counterpart Harrison Butker converted a field

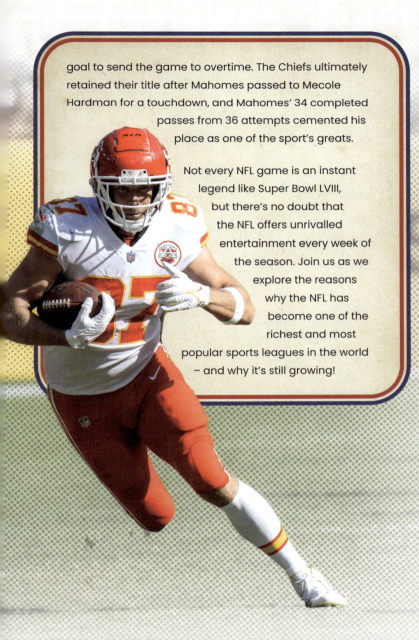

goal to send the game to overtime. The Chiefs ultimately retained their title after Mahomes passed to Mecole Hardman for a touchdown, and Mahomes' 34 completed passes from 36 attempts cemented his place as one of the sport's greats.

Not every NFL game is an instant legend like Super Bowl LVIII, but there's no doubt that the NFL offers unrivalled entertainment every week of the season. Join us as we explore the reasons why the NFL has become one of the richest and most popular sports leagues in the world – and why it's still growing!

1 ANY GIVEN SUNDAY

★★★★★★★★★★★★★★★★★★★★

ANY GIVEN SUNDAY

It doesn't matter whether you're a fan of the reigning Super Bowl champions or the team with the worst regular season record – the **NFL** is designed around establishing parity between its 32 teams. Though individual franchises have dominated and defined particular eras in the sport's history, no team can be counted out for good, even if a period of rebuilding is in order. Parity is the name of the game on a week-to-week basis too, and even the best teams occasionally slip to defeat to an unfancied opponent. That's why only one team has ever gone through an entire season unbeaten.

A typical NFL game lasts almost three hours once the regulation 60 minutes, half-time, two-minute warnings, timeouts and stoppages are taken into account. Still, that doesn't stop many fans from arriving at the stadium hours before kick-off to take part in a pre-game parking-lot ritual that for many is as important as what goes on inside the stadium itself. Tailgating takes its name from what Brits call a car boot. When tailgaters arrive at the stadium, they find a vacant spot on a voluminous tarmac car park, open up the rear of their car and unpack all the equipment needed for a party: foldable tables, a hearty spread of food, a cooler filled with drinks and anything else deemed necessary for a good time.

Some veteran tailgaters light up a **barbecue**, others hook up a big-screen television to watch the pre-match coverage. Selling food and merchandise is frowned upon – instead, it's all about sharing and community. Whatever form a tailgate takes, this NFL ritual is all about sharing your passion for your team and the NFL with regular buddies and like-minded fans – even if they wear opposition colours.

Although the National Football League has existed since 1922 when the two-year-old American Professional Football Association was renamed, the NFL that we know today was only formed in 1970. After decades of operating without any major rivals, the NFL monopoly was threatened in 1960 with the birth of a new pro league: the American Football League. The **AFL** not only operated pro football franchises in American cities that didn't have an NFL team, it also set up teams in cities that already had an NFL presence.

Though many predicted the new league would soon fold like other rival leagues that had come and gone, the AFL proved to be better run than anything that had gone before. It introduced new innovations like player names on jerseys, a game clock prominently displayed on scoreboards and two-point conversions. College prospects were forced to choose which league they preferred to join – and many chose the young upstart rather than the established giant. It soon became clear that the messy situation would only be solved by an NFL-AFL merger. The two leagues began to co-operate from 1966 by holding a joint championship game – the Super Bowl – and a common draft. In 1970, they officially merged under the NFL banner.

4

JOE COOL

★★★★★★★★★★★★★★

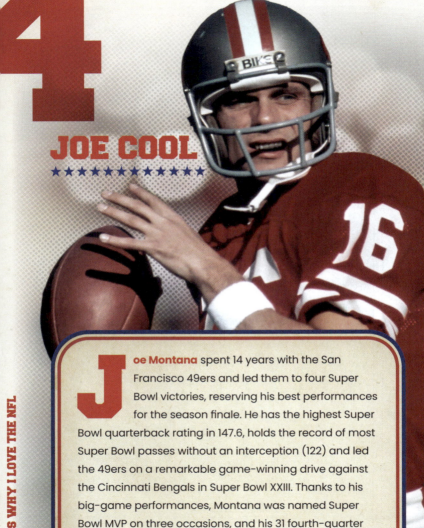

Joe Montana spent 14 years with the San Francisco 49ers and led them to four Super Bowl victories, reserving his best performances for the season finale. He has the highest Super Bowl quarterback rating in 147.6, holds the record of most Super Bowl passes without an interception (122) and led the 49ers on a remarkable game-winning drive against the Cincinnati Bengals in Super Bowl XXIII. Thanks to his big-game performances, Montana was named Super Bowl MVP on three occasions, and his 31 fourth-quarter comebacks mean he is commonly regarded the most clutch quarterback in NFL history.

LONG SNAPPERS

Few positions on the field are as unheralded, but as important, as the long snapper. Their only responsibility is to snap the ball when the punter or field goal kicker is on the field, but it's a surprisingly technical skill. The **long snapper** must throw the ball backwards between their legs. It must travel 15 metres in around 0.7 seconds. It must be perfectly aimed to the punter or holder's hands, and it must be delivered in a spiral so it's immediately in the right orientation for the kick. Given all this, it's no surprise that many wannabe long snappers now attend specialist training camps.

During the offseason, fans of every NFL team have an opportunity to look to the future with optimism as representatives from all 32 franchises converge in the city of one of the teams. Their job is to decide where the best young players in the college system will ply their trade in the NFL. The players themselves get very little choice – by declaring their eligibility for the **draft**, they surrender themselves to the wish of the league. Instead, the teams thrash out who goes where.

To keep the NFL broadly equal, the team with the worst record the season before gets first choice, then the team with the next worst record, all the way through until the Super Bowl champions, who have the last pick. Then, they repeat the process over six more rounds. To complicate matters, teams can trade picks, and compensatory picks are given to teams who lost players in free agency. Though each pick is made amid glitz and glamour on a stage in front of television cameras, the hard work is done behind the scenes. Each team's coaches, scouts and analysts meet in a war room, adapting their strategy as the draft board changes with each pick.

The Cleveland Browns' victory over the New York Jets on 21 September 1970 was a great game – the Browns outscored the Jets 31-21 thanks to a 94-yard kick-off return and a pick-six interception in the fourth quarter. It was the perfect game to launch a new slot in the NFL schedule: ***Monday Night Football***. NFL management had wanted an extra televised game to branch out from Sundays for some time, and the merger between the AFL and NFL proved the perfect time to renegotiate broadcast contracts.

ABC agreed to show one game a week during prime time on Monday nights, extending the weekend and giving fans across the nation one last football fix before the midweek break. Since then, *Monday Night Football* has screened more than 800 games, often the most-fancied match-up of the week. Top commentators, pundits and celebrities ramp up the pre-game hype. Viewership is focused on just one game, meaning that *Monday Night Football* regularly records some of the highest viewing figures in the USA. The prestigious slot remained the property of ABC until 2006, when ESPN put in a superior bid and *Monday Night Football* went to its cable network.

8

THE WRONG WAY RUN

Minnesota Vikings defensive end **Jim Marshall** was an expert at recovering fumbles – he snaffled 29 of them during his career – but people only ever remember the time that 49ers receiver Billy Kilmer was stripped of the ball in October 1964. Marshall picked up the bobbling football and set off for the end zone, running 66 yards without a single opponent getting near him. But there was a reason Marshall was unchallenged – he was running the wrong way. Marshall threw the ball in celebration, giving away a safety, and only realised something was wrong when a 49ers player congratulated him.

THE KICK-OFF GAME

The NFL season officially begins on the Thursday after Labor Day when the defending Super Bowl champions usually host the season opener in a nationally televised game. The schedule organisers try to choose a tasty encounter involving a long-established rivalry – the 2016 opener had the two teams that contested the previous Super Bowl, and just like in the championship game, the **Denver Broncos** defeated the **Carolina Panthers**. The reigning champions usually come out on top, but it's not guaranteed – the Chiefs, Giants, Patriots, Rams and Ravens are among those to have fallen at the first hurdle after winning the Super Bowl.

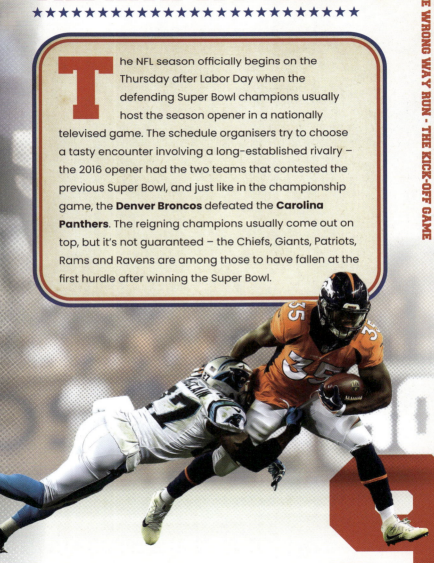

Cheerleading is a mainstay of American culture, and just like the players on the pitch, NFL cheerleaders are the cream of the crop. NFL cheer squads are best known for performing on the sidelines, but there's far more to it than waving a pom-pom. NFL cheerleaders are mostly part-time professionals, often local college students, who've been learning their craft since they were children. Squads train for hours every week to learn choreographed dance moves. Cheerleaders are public representatives of the team.

They attend schools, businesses, conferences and charity events, and many teams ask their cheerleaders to act as mentors on junior cheerleading programmes. Not all NFL franchises embrace the cheer effect, however. The Cleveland Browns and New York Giants have never had a cheerleading squad, while others have dismantled theirs amid criticism that cheerleading is sexist and outdated. However, some teams have tried to bring cheer into the 21st century by appointing male and transgender cheerleaders to their squads, and a representative from each of the 24 remaining cheer teams is selected to perform at the annual Pro Bowl. Gimme a G, gimme an O, go cheerleaders!

11

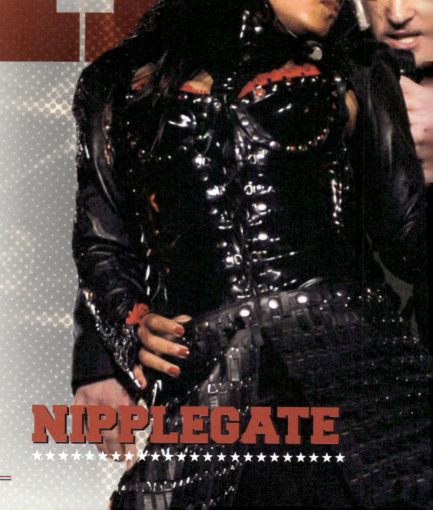

NIPPLEGATE
★★★★★★★★★★★★★★★★★★★★★★★★★★

101 REASONS WHY I LOVE THE NFL

Television viewers watching the Super Bowl XXXVIII half-time show got an eyeful when **Justin Timberlake** sidled up to **Janet Jackson**, singing the final line of his smash hit 'Rock Your Body': 'Gonna have you naked by the end of this song.' He was kind of right. Timberlake pulled Jackson's costume and it came off in his hand, revealing her right breast covered by a sun-shaped nipple shield. The television director immediately cut to a wide shot, but it wasn't enough to stop the United States going into meltdown.

Timberlake and Jackson explained that the planned move was supposed to reveal a red bra – but the bra tore too. They apologised for the 'wardrobe malfunction', coining a new term that soon made it into the dictionary, but some suspicious minds thought that Nipplegate was a deliberate publicity stunt, perhaps because Timberlake wanted to upstage ex-girlfriend Britney Spears who kissed Madonna at the MTV Awards. Jackson herself argued that the media furore was hyped up to distract the American public from the ongoing Iraq War. Whatever the reason for the scandal, Timberlake was invited back to perform at the Super Bowl LII half-time show – this time with no nipple slips.

12

THE REFRIGERATOR

★★★★★★★★★★★★★★★★★★★★

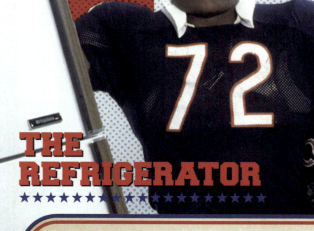

William Perry was a man-mountain. By the time he was 11, he already weighed 90 kilograms – but he was unnaturally fast for a big guy, and coaches saw his potential as an anchor on the defensive line. Perry ended up being a first round pick for the Chicago Bears in 1985, and his instantly recognisable physique – 6 feet 2 inches and 150 kilograms – earned him the nickname 'The Refrigerator'. Perry also lined up as fullback when his offense was inches from the line, and he bulldozered over the line to become the heaviest person to score a touchdown when the Bears won Super Bowl XX.

101 REASONS WHY I LOVE THE NFL

THE FRANCHISE TAG

Nothing can kill a team's prospects more than when a keystone player departs for another team. To prevent this, a team can assign the franchise tag to an impending free agent, preventing another team from making an offer for one year — but the franchise tag comes at a cost. The designated player must be paid either the average of the top five salaries in that player's position, or **120 per cent of their current salary** — whichever is greater. The franchise tag is usually a last option, since its use often causes resentment from players who are barred from testing the market in free agency.

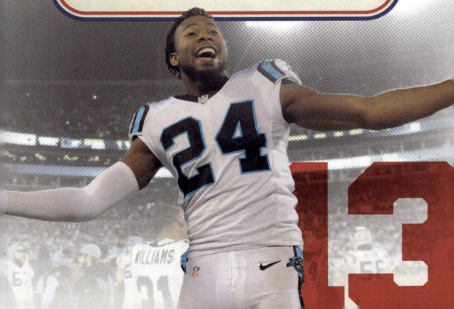

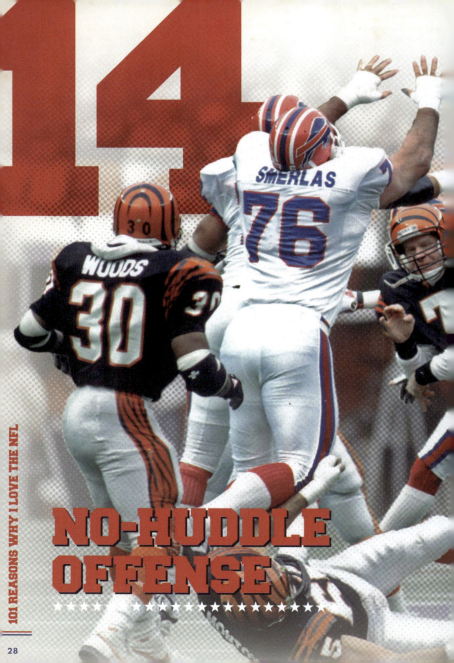

Before each play, offense and defence gather in a huddle on their side of the ball to decide what they'll do on the next play. Beginning in the late 1980s, the **Cincinnati Bengals** mixed things up a bit with the no-huddle offense. By going straight to the line of scrimmage, the Bengals denied the defence a chance to swap players or communicate with the sidelines. In the no-huddle offense, teams usually line up in a set formation for a series of predetermined plays. They might snap the ball quickly, hoping to catch the defence out of position.

Alternatively, the quarterback might call an audible to alter the play choice depending on what he sees – and a quarterback who really wants to outfox the opposition might keep his team in position as the play clock counts down, calling repeated audibles which may be real, or may be fake. After being defeated by the Bengals' pioneering no-huddle offense in the 1988 AFC Championship Game, the Buffalo Bills took it to a new level. The early 1990s Bills often went no-huddle for the entire game, placing responsibility for play calls on quarterback Jim Kelly – and it helped them win four consecutive AFC Championships.

After 30 years and one Super Bowl victory, the relationship between the Baltimore Colts and their home city broke down following the 1983 season. For more than a decade, the local authorities had tried to increase the rent at Memorial Stadium, but the Colts refused to pay more until the city improved the antiquated facility. The standoff went on for years, escalating as Baltimore politicians blocked plans for a brand-new stadium and Colts owner Robert Irsay openly shopped his team across the country.

When Irsay's fellow NFL owners gave him permission to move to a city of his choosing, the writing was on the wall – Baltimore was going to lose its NFL team. Baltimore politicians reacted with fury, threatening to seize Irsay's assets and take control of the franchise. The following evening, a fleet of trucks arrived at Memorial Stadium. When Baltimoreans woke the next morning, they were heartbroken to find out that their team had left them in the middle of the night and relocated the city that offered Irsay the best deal: **Indianapolis**. After enduring 12 years without pro football, Baltimoreans gained a new team to support when the Ravens were formed as an expansion team.

16
THE FIRST-DOWN LINE

★★★★★★★★★★★★★★★★

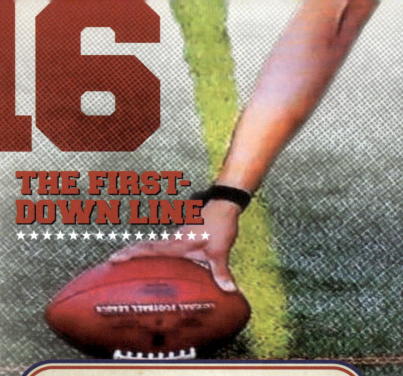

To retain possession of the ball, an offense must advance ten yards in four downs – but it's not always easy to see exactly where the ten-yard target is. That problem was solved for NFL television viewers in 1998, when ESPN started displaying a **virtual yellow line** on the field marking the spot the offense needed to reach. The line was a clever bit of computer wizardry, but many of the first viewers were bamboozled by the technology and thought it was a physical line that was moved during drive. Now, it's almost impossible to imagine football on TV without this clever bit of kit.

THE DIRTY BIRD DANCE

★★★★★★★★★★★★★★★★★★★★★★★★★★★★★★

The 1998 Atlanta Falcons scored 46 touchdowns, giving them plenty of opportunities to perfect an iconic celebration. The **Dirty Bird** was first performed by running back Jamal Anderson in Week 6. He dived into the end zone, jumped up and started flapping his arms while hopping from side to side. Soon, fans were stopping the Falcons on the street to perform their own rendition of the Dirty Bird as the Falcons went all the way to the Super Bowl. Since then, dozens of Anderson's successors have happily flapped their way through the end zone at the Georgia Dome and Mercedes-Benz Stadium.

17

18

THE SCHEDULE FORMULA

★★★★★★★★★★★★★★★★★★★★★★

101 REASONS WHY I LOVE THE NFL

The NFL has 32 **teams** split over two conferences and eight divisions – and each team plays 17 games a season. It all adds up to a nightmare for the fixture planners, who have to ensure that each team gets a fair crack at making the playoffs. To make the schedule impartial and reduce the power of an individual's bias, a complex formula has been devised. Each team plays twice against the other three teams in its division – once at home, once away. They also play once against the four teams from another division within their conference, and once against the four teams from another division in the other conference. That leaves three empty slots in the schedule.

Two are filled by matching up the teams from the same conference that finished in the same position in their division the year before. The recently added 17th game pitches a team against an opponent from the other conference that finished in the same position in their division. Is it confusing? Absolutely! But it's also a fair system that gives each team a chance for success while ensuring there are some great matchups every week of the regular season.

19

THE 12s
★★★★★★★★★★★★★★★

101 REASONS WHY I LOVE THE NFL

At the end of the 1984 regular season, the Seattle Seahawks honoured their fans by retiring the number 12 jersey – a nod to the common sporting anecdote that their fans act as the team's 12th man. Unfortunately, the fans didn't return the favour. For most of the 1990s, the Seahawks played in front of part-empty stadiums and the franchise owner even considered relocating to Los Angeles. However, Hawks fans came flocking back when their team began to challenge for the NFC West title under coaches Mike Holmgren and Pete Carroll. In 2003, when Seahawks Stadium opened, a giant flagpole was erected at the south end for a new pre-game ceremony: raising a giant blue and green flag with the number 12 on it.

Since then, the **12 flag** has become a symbol of the team, displayed atop Seattle's Space Needle and even at the summit of Mount Everest. The new Seahawks Stadium was also designed to funnel crowd noise onto the field. Seahawks fans twice broke the world record for loudest crowd noise at a sporting event during the 2013 season, and their celebrations for a Marshawn Lynch touchdown in 2010 even registered on a nearby seismograph.

20 THE SNOW PLOW GAME

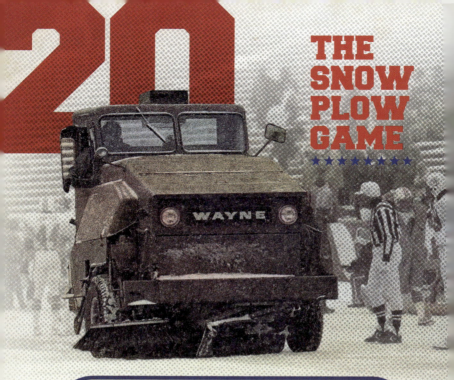

New England is famed for its wintery weather, and the Miami Dolphins found themselves frozen in a stalemate in their December 1982 game visit to the Patriots. The snow fell so heavily that the officials called for a drive-on **snowplow** to help clear the yard markers, and when the Patriots had a field goal attempt in the game's dying minutes, head coach Ron Meyer ordered the driver to clear a spot for the kicker to use. The kick was good, the Patriots won 3–0, and the frigid Dolphins were left bemoaning the home team's snowplow advantage.

THE RED ZONE

As a team nears an opponent's end zone, it breaches the **red zone** – the area of the field between the goal line and 20-yard line. Tension ramps up as the chance of scoring increases. Passes don't need to travel as far and a missed tackle can lead to a touchdown. But the offense doesn't get everything its own way – defensive backs have a smaller area to defend and passes have a greater risk of being intercepted. In recent years, offensive co-ordinators have been judged on whether their team can get it done through statistical analysis of their team's success in the red zone.

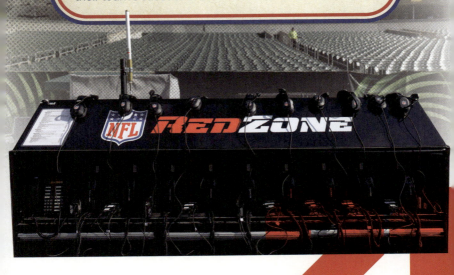

Over 25,000 men have played in the NFL since it was created in 1920 – but less than 400 have been deemed worthy of inclusion in the **Pro Football Hall of Fame**. This institution based in Canton, Ohio, records the deeds of the NFL's most exceptional characters. The vast majority are players, but there's also room for the coaches, executives and broadcasters who've left their mark on the game. Among the inaugural class of 1963 were running backs Red Grange and Jim Thorpe, and Chicago Bears owner and coach George Halas. Since then, they've been joined by luminaries like Vince Lombardi (1971), Joe Montana (2000) and Peyton Manning (2021).

Each year, between four and eight new inductees are selected by a 48-man committee. Consideration is only given to people who've been retired for at least five years and were active in the last 40 years. A separate nine-man seniors committee puts forward two names from previously overlooked players whose contributions to the sport came prior to 1985. The enshrinement ceremony is a week-long festival that kicks off with a pre-season game and ends with each new inductee receiving a gold jacket and unveiling their bust in the Hall of Fame building.

23

101 REASONS WHY I LOVE THE NFL

WORLD

★★★★★★★★★★★★★★★★

nicknamed 'World' because there was no ball in the world that he couldn't catch, **Jerry Rice** burst onto the scene with the San Francisco 49ers in 1985 and quickly established himself as the greatest wide receiver in NFL history – and in some people's opinion, the greatest player in NFL history full stop. He led the league in receiving yards six times and receiving touchdowns six times. His 22 touchdown receptions in 1987 was a single-season record at the time, and came despite a strike-shortened 12-game regular season.

Rice earned three Super Bowl rings – the first of which saw him named Super Bowl MVP – and was twice named the Offensive Player of the Year. Some receivers build a rapport with a particular quarterback and struggle to maintain the same form when an alternative comes in. Not Rice. He was equally at home catching passes from Steve Young as he was with Joe Montana. No wide receiver has played longer than his 20 seasons, and two decades on from his retirement, Rice still holds the NFL records for receptions, receiving yards, receiving touchdowns, total touchdowns and total yards – and has scored more points than any player other than kickers.

24

THE MUSIC CITY MIRACLE

It should have been all over for the Tennessee Titans when the Buffalo Bills kicked a field goal near the end of the AFC Wild Card Game in 2000. There were only 16 seconds left in the game, and the Bills kicked off with a 16-15 lead. Most expected the Titans to get the ball across the sideline to stop the clock and attempt a Hail Mary, but the Titans had a special play up their sleeve. Fullback Lorenzo Neal received the kick-off. He handed the ball to tight end Frank Wycheck, who threw a lateral to wide receiver **Kevin Dyson**, who raced up the sideline for the game-winning touchdown.

PRACTICE SQUADS

★★★★★★★★★★★★★★★★★★★★★★★★★★★

NFL rosters are big, with 53 players at any one time being contracted to the team and available to play – but sometimes that's not enough. With so many specialist positions, each role is normally only covered by one or two backups who can be slotted into the lineup when injuries strike or a player drops out of form. That's where the **practice squad** comes into play. This cohort of 16 players trains with the team, serve as extra backups, and can be called up on game days – but other teams are also free to poach practice squad players to fill their own gaps.

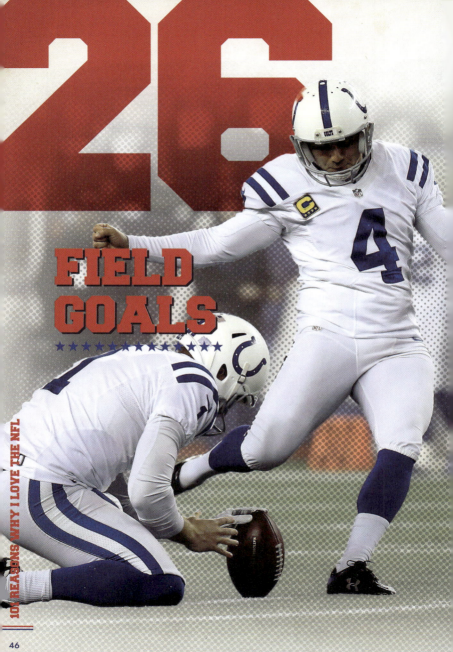

Sometimes an offense will decide it's not worth the risk of losing the ball on downs, and forgo the chance of a touchdown to kick a field goal through the uprights instead. The reward isn't as great – three points instead of a touchdown's six (seven with the extra point) – but the chances of scoring are far higher and the best NFL kickers have a success rate in the high 90 per cent range. Gary Anderson converted every single one of his 35 field goal attempts with the 1998 Baltimore Ravens, and including his carried-over streak from the end of the 1997 season, he had 46 consecutive field goals. But kickers can never forget the pressure that goes with every single kick.

Anderson's streak came to an end when he missed a field goal in the NFC Championship Game. It was a decisive miss. The game went to overtime, the Atlanta Falcons won, and the Ravens missed out on the Super Bowl. Kickers can be matchwinners as well as match losers. **Adam Vinatieri** had the privilege of kicking two Super Bowl-winning field goals for the New England Patriots en route to becoming the most successful kicker of all time with 2,673 points.

27

THE DRIVE

101 REASONS WHY I LOVE THE NFL

THE DRIVE

NFL officials on the sidelines at Cleveland Stadium in 1987 were so sure that the Browns were about to progress to their first Super Bowl that they took the AFC Championship trophy to the home dressing room in anticipation. The Browns had just gone 20-13 up with five minutes to go, and their opponents – the Denver Broncos – had botched the kick-off return. Broncos quarterback **John Elway** took over on his own two-yard line with almost the entire field to cover. What followed next was a clutch performance that's known simply as The Drive. Elway barely wasted a moment. He moved his team up the field in seven plays, every single one of which gained yards, to reach the halfway line by the two-minute warning.

The Broncos then briefly stuttered with an incomplete pass and a quarterback sack before launching a 20-yard passing play. They moved further into Browns territory with more passes to get to the five-yard line, before Elway passed to Mark Jackson to tie the game with 39 seconds remaining. The Broncos went on to win in overtime, and the Browns would have to wait until their first Super Bowl appearance. They're still waiting, more than 35 years later.

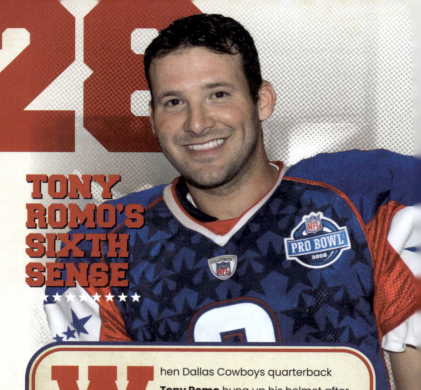

TONY ROMO'S SIXTH SENSE

When Dallas Cowboys quarterback **Tony Romo** hung up his helmet after 14 seasons, he was quickly signed up by CBS as a colour commentator for their televised games. He brought his recent experience as a starting QB to the broadcasting booth, demonstrating his ability to read formations in a split-second and predict offensive plays and defensive strategies before the ball was snapped. Romostradmus' ability to call plays has declined the longer he's out of the game, but his enthusiasm and rapport with play-by-play caller Jim Nantz means that the CBS crew is often considered the best broadcast team in North American sports.

REVENUE SHARING

★★★★★★★★★★★★★★★★★★★★★★★

The NFL includes the richest sports team in the world – **the Dallas Cowboys** – but league bosses try to keep the teams on a relatively level playing field by sharing revenue generated on a national scale. That means money generated by television deals, merchandising, league sponsorship and a proportion of ticket sales is put into a pot and divided up equally between all 32 teams, regardless of whether the money is generated in giant New York or tiny Green Bay. Thanks to national revenue sharing, each team receives more than $300 million each year to help pay salaries and market their team.

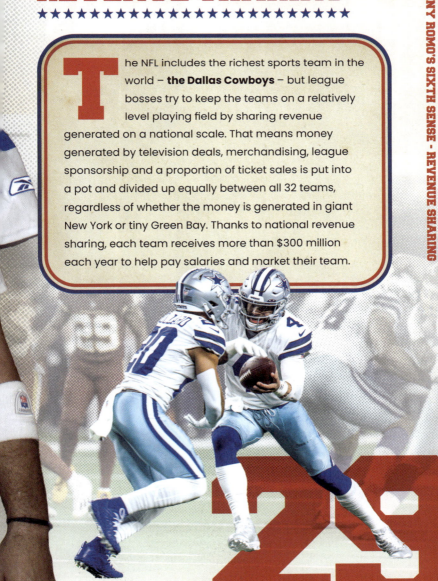

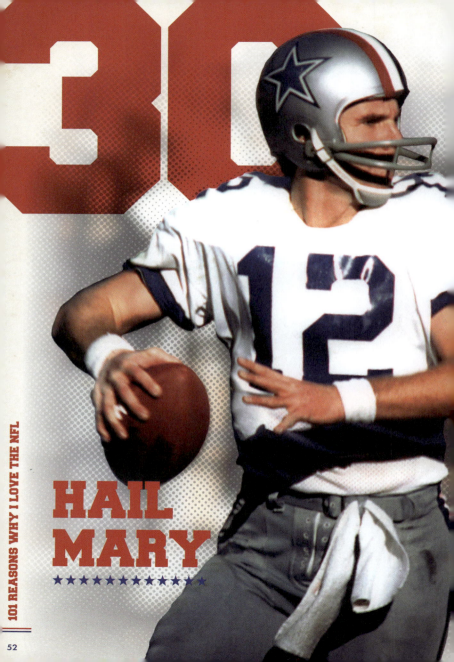

HAIL MARY

As its name suggests, the Hail Mary is only brought out when a team is in need of divine intervention: a few points down but far from the end zone with time for one more play. The only way to win is with a long pass, flung in the vain hope that it might be caught in the end zone. The idea of the Hail Mary gained widespread use after Dallas Cowboys quarterback **Roger Staubach** threw a 50-yard pass to Drew Pearson in the last few seconds of a game against the Minnesota Vikings in December 1975. In the postgame press conference, Staubach admitted: 'I closed my eyes and said a Hail Mary.'

Since then, a Hail Mary gave the Cleveland Browns their first victory as an expansion franchise in 1999. Three years later, Tim Couch became the only NFL quarterback to win two games through Hail Marys when the Browns beat the Jacksonville Jaguars. But perhaps the greatest Hail Mary came when Aaron Rodgers threw a 61-yard pass against the Detroit Lions to claim a win for the Green Bay Packers. It was the longest Hail Mary in NFL history and soon became dubbed the Miracle in Motown.

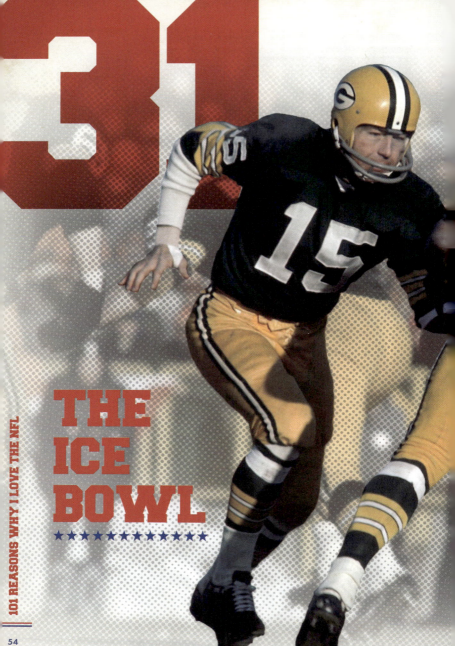

THE ICE BOWL

The 1967 NFL Championship Game matched up the two teams that contested the title the previous year: the Green Bay Packers and Dallas Cowboys. It soon became clear that the rematch would be a sub-zero battle. Lambeau Field was stuck in -26 degree Celsius temperatures, and wind chill pushed it even lower. When the ground crew removed a tarpaulin from the pitch, they discovered the under-pitch heating had malfunctioned, and a layer of water had frozen solid on the turf. The game began with the referee's lips sticking to the whistle, and the officials spent the rest of the game shouting to end each play.

Both teams handled the ball well despite the cold, and the Cowboys took a 17-14 lead on a 50-yard trick play early in the fourth quarter. With five minutes to go, the Packers had one last chance and began a drive downfield that ended on the one-yard line with seconds remaining. Quarterback **Bart Starr** called a rushing play he was supposed to hand off to his fullback, but he chose to lunge for the goal line himself for the game-winning score. The Ice Bowl, as the game soon became known, entered NFL lore as the last great game before the AFL merger.

32

BABY GOAT
★★★★★★★★

101 REASONS WHY I LOVE THE NFL

The Kansas City Chiefs have enjoyed unprecedented success since selecting quarterback **Patrick Mahomes** in the 2017 draft. Mahomes led his team to the AFC Championship Game in each of his first six seasons as starter, going on to win three Super Bowl rings. Mahomes is a dynamic player, able to keep a play going as his offensive line collapses thanks to his ability throw the ball accurately while on the run – his highlight reel includes no-look passes and behind-the-back tosses. If he can maintain his stunning early-career success, Mahomes might be in the running for the title of Greatest Player of All Time.

QUARTERBACK SACKS

Defensive ends, as their name suggests, line up at the end of the line of scrimmage. Nothing pleases these speedy but brutal ruffians more than bypassing their offensive counterpart and tackling the quarterback for a loss. In the 1960s, Hall of Famer **Deacon Jones** began referring to his QB tackles as 'sacks', and the term caught on. A timely sack pushes the line of scrimmage back, meaning that a team must gain even more yards for a first down. Bruce Smith holds the NFL record with 200 sacks over his career, while Derrick Thomas had seven in one game for the Kansas City Chiefs in 1990.

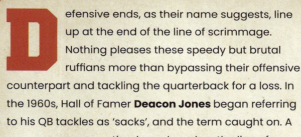

33

BABY GOAT · QUARTERBACK SACKS

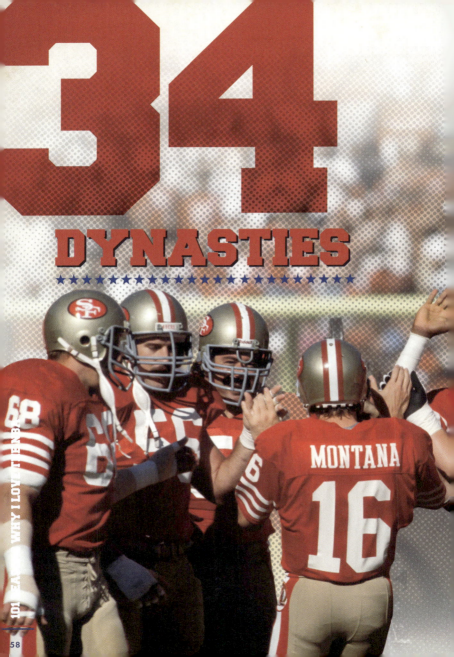

34
DYNASTIES

DYNASTIES

The egalitarian nature of North American sports is supposed to prevent one team topping the league for an extended period – but that hasn't stopped certain teams dominating a particular era. These dynasties, as American sports fans like to call them, tend to share a few common factors: an elite head coach, a Hall of Fame quarterback, and a selection of offensive and defensive weapons to call upon. The Super Bowl era dawned as the Green Bay Packers dynasty of Vince Lombardi was coming to an end, but that didn't stop the team winning Super Bowls I and II.

Since then, the 'Steel Curtain' defence made the Pittsburgh Steelers into the team of the 1970s, with eight consecutive playoff appearances leading to four Super Bowl titles in six years. Joe Montana's **San Francisco 49ers** ruled the 1980s with four Super Bowl titles over the decade, and the Dallas Cowboys won three titles in four years in the 1990s. More recently, the New England Patriots have been the team to beat in the 21st century. Over an unprecedented two decades, the Patriots won six Super Bowls, had three losing Super Bowl appearances, and won their division 17 times in 19 years.

MADDEN NFL

In 1984, video game maker Electronic Arts approached NFL coach and broadcaster **John Madden** with a proposal: they wanted him to endorse their new football game and provide a playbook that players could choose from. Madden agreed, but only if the game was realistic. He refused to back the initial version, which only had six or seven players per team. Instead, EA's programmers were forced to rewrite the code to allow 11-a-side games on primitive 1980s computers, but their extra work was worthwhile and *John Madden Football* – eventually released in 1988 – proved to be a hit. Since then, new releases have gradually honed the game's graphics, realism and playability.

The annual unveiling of the game's cover is a big media event, though many believe the existence of the Madden curse, in which the previous year's cover star suffers a drop in form or an injury. *Madden NFL* (as the games were renamed in 1994) has sold more than one hundred million copies and generated billions of dollars in revenue. Fans who grew up in the 1990s and beyond are more likely to know John Madden as the face of a video game rather than a Super Bowl-winning head coach and top broadcaster.

36 INSTANT REPLAY

★★★★★★★★★★★★★

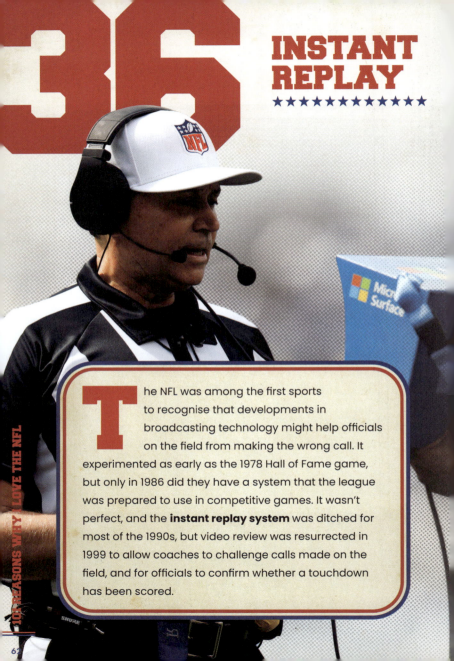

The NFL was among the first sports to recognise that developments in broadcasting technology might help officials on the field from making the wrong call. It experimented as early as the 1978 Hall of Fame game, but only in 1986 did they have a system that the league was prepared to use in competitive games. It wasn't perfect, and the **instant replay system** was ditched for most of the 1990s, but video review was resurrected in 1999 to allow coaches to challenge calls made on the field, and for officials to confirm whether a touchdown has been scored.

END ZONE MILITIA

★★★★★★★★★★★★★★★★★★★★★★★★★

No team has breached their opponent's end zone more in recent years than the New England Patriots, so it's convenient that the Patriots introduced a new act to help them celebrate in 1996, just before their period of sustained success began. The **End Zone Militia** is a group of 20 historical reenactors who dress as though they've just walked out of the War of Independence. They entertain the crowd before the game begins, and after kick-off, assemble behind each end zone in anticipation of a Patriots score. Every time their team does shift the scoreboard, the militia fires blanks from their muskets in celebration.

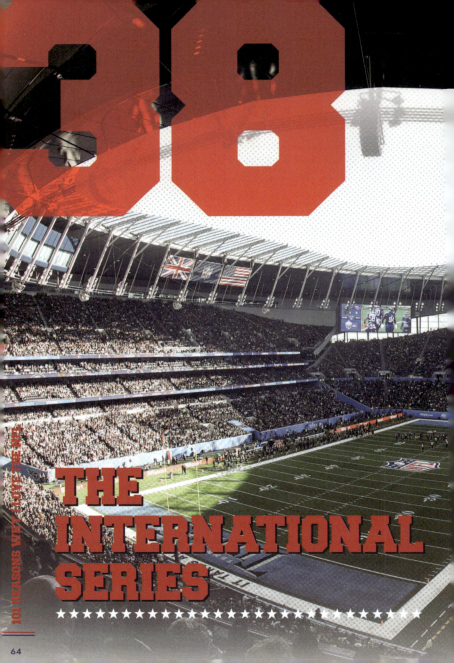

38

THE INTERNATIONAL SERIES

101 REASONS WHY... I LOVE THE NFL

THE INTERNATIONAL SERIES

As its name suggests, American football is largely restricted to the United States. For the rest of the world, 'football' means a completely different sport, but that hasn't stopped the NFL looking to expand beyond its borders. In the 1990s, NFL bosses tried to establish a European version of the NFL, but it never really took off. European fans didn't want a watered-down development league – they wanted the real thing. They got what they wanted in 2007, when NFL regular season games began to take place outside the United States – initially in **London**, then Mexico, and most recently Germany and Brazil.

The International Series has seen every franchise play in unfamiliar surroundings, but no team has travelled more than the Jacksonville Jaguars. They've flashed their passports to British border guards every year since 2013 (apart from 2020, when Covid-19 made international travel impossible). Despite the difficulties of adjusting to a new time zone, most players enjoy the experience of playing in front of foreign fans. The International Series has been so well supported that the next step is a postseason contest held beyond America's borders – perhaps even an international Super Bowl – or a franchise based on the other side of the Atlantic.

39

101 REASONS WHY I LOVE THE NFL

CHEESEHEADS

As the NFL franchise based in the smallest city – population 107,000 – the Green Bay Packers don't have a huge demographic to draw upon. Thankfully, a combination of history and tradition ensures that the Packers have as dedicated a fanbase as any other franchise. Thanks to Wisconsin's reputation as America's dairy, Packers fans are affectionately known as **Cheeseheads**. They've adopted a tricorn-shaped cheese hat first used by fans of the Milwaukee Brewers baseball team. The first version was made by a Brewers fan using foam from his mother's sofa, and the entrepreneurial fan turned the novelty into a multi-million-dollar business.

In 1995, a cheesehead hat saved the life a Packers fan who was involved in a plane crash when returning home after watching the Packers play the Cleveland Browns. The fan suffered a broken ankle but was supposedly saved from a severe head injury due to the padding in his hat. Thanks to the dedication of the Cheeseheads, every Packers home game has been sold out since 1960, and they have one of the longest season ticket waiting lists in professional sports – a new fan can expect to wait thirty years before they reach the front of the queue.

40

DAN ORLOVSKY'S SAFETY

★★★★★★★★★★★★★★★★★★★★★★★★

Detroit Lions backup quarterback **Dan Orlovsky** had a game to forget when he was finally called upon for his first game as starter, against the Minnesota Vikings in 2008. Early in the first quarter, with the ball on the Lions' one-yard line, Orlovsky lined up in shotgun formation. When the ball was snapped, he backpedalled – but he ran outside the end zone to concede a two-point safety. What made the gaffe even worse was that the Lions ultimately lost 12-10 without the chance to go to overtime, and it was the closest the Lions came to victory in a historic 0-16 winless season.

WILD CARD WEEKEND

★★★★★★★★★★★★★★★★★★★★★★★★★★★

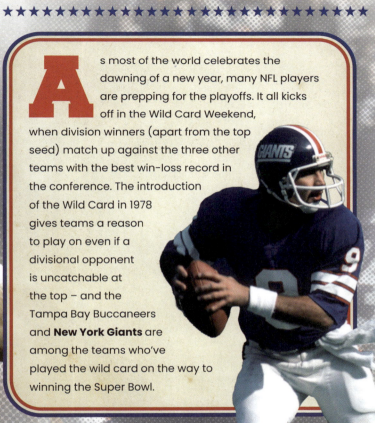

As most of the world celebrates the dawning of a new year, many NFL players are prepping for the playoffs. It all kicks off in the Wild Card Weekend, when division winners (apart from the top seed) match up against the three other teams with the best win-loss record in the conference. The introduction of the Wild Card in 1978 gives teams a reason to play on even if a divisional opponent is uncatchable at the top – and the Tampa Bay Buccaneers and **New York Giants** are among the teams who've played the wild card on the way to winning the Super Bowl.

KICK-OFF RETURNS

For most of its history, football games have begun with a simple kick-off to the opposing team. An opposing player catches the ball and tries to gain as many yards as possible before a wall of defenders envelopes him. The idea is to gain as good field position as possible – the fewer yards a quarterback has to drive his team downfield, the more likely they are to score. In recent years, kick-off returns have been made safer.

The receiving team can call for a fair catch and begin at the 25-yard line, no matter where the ball is caught, lowering the risk of concussions as teams charge at each other from distance. Still, a receiver will sometimes gamble and run the gauntlet as he tries to gain a better starting location. Sometimes it goes wrong and he's tackled for a loss, but if he finds a gap and gets some good blocks from his teammates, he might run it all the way back for a touchdown. Nobody did it better than wide receiver and returns specialist **Devin Hester**, who had 20 kick-off and punt touchdown returns over his career, including a 90-yarder on the opening kick-off of Super Bowl XLI.

DEFLATEGATE

When the 2014 New England Patriots made their fourth consecutive appearance in the AFC Championship Game, their infamous attention to detail led to them breaking the rules – at least according to the NFL. After intercepting a pass, Indianapolis Colts linebacker D'Qwell Jackson thought the ball was suspiciously soft. At half-time, the officials tested the balls and found some of them were indeed lower than permitted. The balls were reinflated, but in the second half, the Patriots scored 28 unanswered points for a comprehensive win. That didn't stop the NFL announcing an investigation into whether the Patriots deliberately deflated balls to give quarterback **Tom Brady** an advantage when gripping the ball.

The Patriots won Super Bowl XLIX two weeks later, but the protracted investigation dragged on. Ultimately, Brady was banned for four games because the NFL judged it 'more probable than not' that Brady was 'generally aware' about the deflated balls. It was hardly a smoking gun. Brady served his suspension at the start of the 2016 season, but he had a chip on his shoulder and led the Patriots through a dominant campaign that ended with NFL Commissioner Roger Goodell being roundly booed when he presented the team with the Vince Lombardi Trophy.

44

THE FREIGHT TRAIN

★★★★★★★★★★★★

Jim Brown played nine seasons with the Cleveland team that shared his name, never missing a game and breaking a host of NFL records. At a time when the NFL was a rush-first game, Brown broke had 2,359 carries, 12,312 rushing yards and 106 touchdowns. His average of 104.3 rushing yards per game remains the highest ever seen in the league and makes him the only player to have over 100 rushing yards per game for his career. Brown suddenly called it a day at the age of 30, having rushed for three touchdowns in the 1966 Pro Bowl, and with nothing left to prove.

101 REASONS WHY I LOVE THE NFL.

DRAFT BUSTS

★★★★★★★★★★★★★★★★★★★

Like car drivers who slow as they pass the scene of an accident, NFL fans get a morbid thrill when they see a rival team push all its chips into the middle of the table and gamble a franchise's future on a single individual – only for the chosen saviour to sink without trace. **JaMarcus Russell** was supposed to turn the fortunes of the Oakland Raiders when he was selected with the number one pick in 2007. After racking up more interceptions than touchdowns over the course of 31 disappointing games, Russell was released before the 2010 season – and no team was interested in taking on the draft bust.

46

BACKUP QUARTERBACKS

101 REASONS WHY I LOVE THE NFL

Backup quarterbacks spend most of their career in the shadows, knowing they're only going to be called upon in a crisis. Sometimes, a backup is summoned when the first-choice quarterback is playing badly. Others are thrown into the arena when the starting QB goes down with an injury. But a reliable backup is a valuable asset. Some teams sign a veteran at the tail-end of their career to mentor a new, young starter. Others want a backup whose style of play is similar to the starter they shadow, so the whole playbook isn't ripped up if the first-choice QB suffers a season-ending injury.

That strategy paid dividends in Philadelphia in 2017, when **Nick Foles** stepped into the breach after Carson Wentz tore an ACL in Week 14. Foles took the Philadelphia Eagles all the way to a Super Bowl win. Often, the backup will be relegated to the bench when the starter is ready to play again, but not always. Tom Brady was given a chance when Drew Bledsoe suffered an injury for the New England Patriots, but by the time Bledsoe was healthy again, Brady was already on the path to becoming the most successful NFL player of all time.

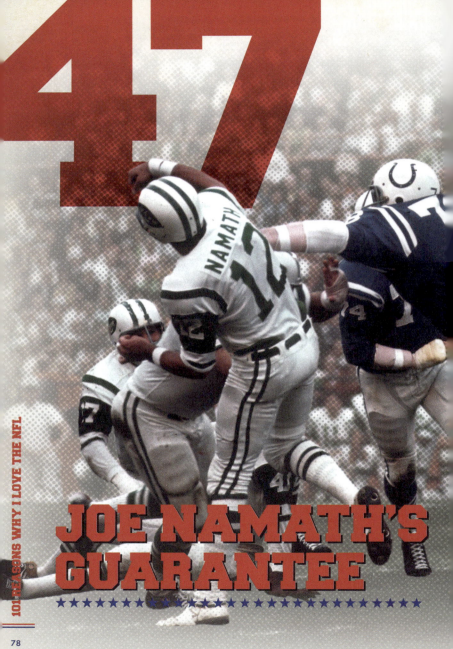

The first two Super Bowls promised to pitch the champion of the long-established NFL with the best of the upstart AFL, but the games themselves were disappointing affairs. The NFL's Green Bay Packers won the first two championships, blasting the Kansas City Chiefs and Oakland Raiders off the park. Most expected Super Bowl III to be a similar walk in the park for the new NFL champions, the Baltimore Colts, and gave the AFL champion New York Jets no chance. But Jets quarterback **Joe Namath** believed in his ability to overturn the odds.

Three days before the big game, Namath attended an end-of-season dinner and was heckled by a Colts fan. Fed up with people dismissing his team, Joe responded to the heckler when he got to the podium: 'We're gonna win the game. I guarantee it.' Although most laughed off his unlikely prediction, Namath backed up his words on the field. He turned in an MVP performance, picking gaps in the Colts defence with a dominant rushing game. The Jets victory wasn't just the crowning moment of Broadway Joe's career – it revitalised an end-of-season championship game that had threatened to become stale and predictable.

48
THE TELESTRATOR

★★★★★★★★★★★★★★★★★★★★

Fans sometimes find it difficult to grasp what's going on in the chaos surrounding the line of scrimmage, but the nuances of plays were easier to understand after Super Bowl XVI in 1982, when John Madden became the first national broadcaster to use a light pen to draw on the television screen. The **telestrator**, as the invention was called, enabled Madden to highlight players of interest on replays, drawing their intended routes and blocks. His freehand scribbles soon became a standard way for colour commentators to communicate their thoughts to the watching audience, and the telestrator is still in use today.

TRICK PLAYS

★★★★★★★★★★★★★★★★★★★

There are tens of thousands of offensive plays out there, but most are variants on the two basic approaches to moving the ball: pass or rush. Occasionally, offensive co-ordinators mix things up a bit by pulling a **trick play** out of the bag. These aim to win easy yards by bamboozling the defence with something unexpected. Some teams pretend to punt but have the kicker rush up the field. Others have the centre snap the ball direct to a running back, or have the quarterback throw a backwards pass to a receiver, who's then free to launch the ball downfield.

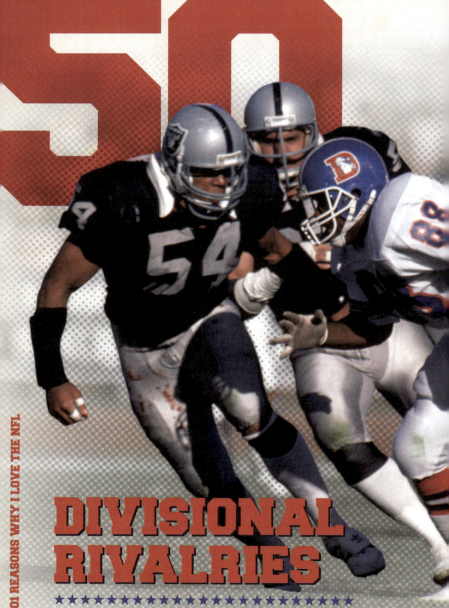

50

DIVISIONAL RIVALRIES

101 REASONS WHY I LOVE THE NFL

DIVISIONAL RIVALRIES

Each season, every NFL team plays the other three teams in its division twice – once at home, once away. These regular matchups mean that the four teams in a division sometimes become fed up with the sight of each other. That's when a divisional rivalry forms. The **Los Angeles Raiders** and **Denver Broncos** have played each other more than 125 times despite the Raiders moving locations several times, and both players and fans of the New England Patriots and New York Jets love to hate each other. Some of the best rivalries have history behind them.

The Green Bay Packers and Chicago Bears have played each other since the early days of the NFL, and the Philadelphia Eagles and Dallas Cowboys have been in the same division since 1961. The Pittsburgh Steelers and Baltimore Ravens rivalry may not have such a long legacy, but these two teams have gone toe-to-toe – and occasionally fist-to-fist – since the Ravens were formed in 1996. Joey Porter and Ray Lewis allegedly began the feud when Porter went after Lewis after a game in 2003, and since then fans from both teams have bought into the ill-feeling. Now, each game between the two teams is hotly anticipated.

THE GOAT

Prior to the 2000 draft, anybody predicting that **Tom Brady** would become the GOAT – the Greatest Of All-Time – would have been laughed from the room. The University of Michigan quarterback was selected with the 199th pick by the New England Patriots and was initially their third-choice QB. He became backup in training camp and took over as starter when Drew Bledsoe suffered internal bleeding after a hard tackle in 2001. Brady took advantage of his sudden promotion, leading the Patriots to an unlikely Super Bowl victory and the first for the franchise. It wasn't the last. During Brady's 20 years in New England, he led the Patriots to 17 AFC East titles, nine AFC Championship titles and six Super Bowl wins.

Brady was a remarkably durable athlete, only suffering one serious injury (a torn ACL that kept him out for almost all of 2008) and carried on playing well after other quarterbacks would have retired. After leaving New England, Brady spent his final three years in Tampa Bay with the Buccaneers, leading them to a Super Bowl win. With seven rings, Brady isn't just the player with the most Super Bowl wins – he's won more than any other team.

52 THE SUPER BOWL SHUFFLE

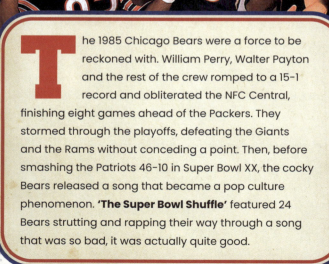

The 1985 Chicago Bears were a force to be reckoned with. William Perry, Walter Payton and the rest of the crew romped to a 15-1 record and obliterated the NFC Central, finishing eight games ahead of the Packers. They stormed through the playoffs, defeating the Giants and the Rams without conceding a point. Then, before smashing the Patriots 46-10 in Super Bowl XX, the cocky Bears released a song that became a pop culture phenomenon. **'The Super Bowl Shuffle'** featured 24 Bears strutting and rapping their way through a song that was so bad, it was actually quite good.

THE TWO-MINUTE DRILL

★★★★★★★★★★★★★★★★★★★★★★★★★★★★★★

Two minutes from the end of each half, the game is halted with a **timeout**. It began in the days before stadiums had game clocks to warn teams that time was about to run out. Now, the two-minute warning often sends an offense into a pre-prepared programme of plays that they can run through without the need to huddle, giving them more chance to move the ball downfield before the clock runs out. When seconds become even more crucial, a quarterback will spike the ball – deliberately throwing it into the ground to stop the clock at the cost of a down.

Since the earliest days of the NFL, **Thanksgiving Day** has seen football played outside of the usual Sunday bracket. The Detroit Lions hosted their first Thanksgiving game in 1934, and the Dallas Cowboys were given a Thanksgiving game in 1966. These two teams still play at home every Thanksgiving, with the Cowboys currently enjoying the better record. Since 2006, a third game has been added to the mix, though there are no fixed teams for this encounter – though plenty of franchises would love the chance to be a regular host since they're popular occasions, usually the fourth-highest viewed games of the season after the Super Bowl and conference championships.

Although the players involved must postpone their own celebrations, they know they'll be playing in front of a national audience and vie to be named the game's top player. The lucky recipients receive a turkey leg on the field as part of the post-game festivities and take a bite out of it for the television cameras. Thanks to the traditions that have grown up around the Thanksgiving game, the annual holiday usually means three things for most Americans: food, family and football.

55

FANTASY FOOTBALL

★★★★★★★★★★★★★★★★★★★★★★★★

101 REASONS WHY I LOVE THE NFL

90

FANTASY FOOTBALL

Football is a game of statistics, which makes it perfect for wannabe head coaches and general managers to live out their dreams in a make-believe league. In **fantasy football** leagues, competitors select an imaginary roster using actual NFL players, often participating in a fantasy draft to ensure that not every team picks the same favoured players. Points are awarded based on each player's real-life performances on the field. Passing yards, rushing yards, tackles, sacks and fumbles all count depending on the fantasy league's scoring system.

As the season progresses, fantasy managers shuffle their rosters to designate new starters depending on which of their players is in form and who their real-life opposition is in the next round of games. Managers can usually trade players between teams, although most systems allow other bosses to veto trades to stop managers collaborating and gaming the system. The temptation to cheat is strong, since many games offer cash prizes to the best-performing teams. In 2022, baseball fans were left confused when two players engaged in fisticuffs on the field of play. It later transpired that the source of the argument was a dispute over a fantasy football league in which both players were competing.

56 RIVER CITY RELAY

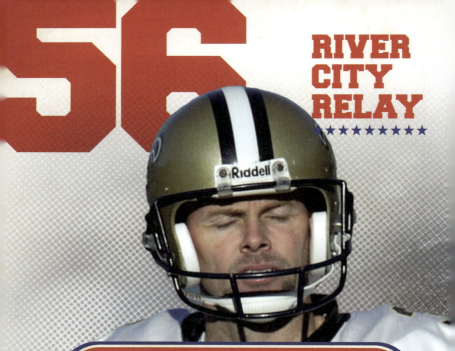

Needing a win to keep their playoffs hopes alive, the New Orleans Saints trailed the Jacksonville Jaguars with seven seconds left in Week 16 of 2003. The clock ticked down to zero as the Saints ran from their 25-yard line into Jaguars territory, throwing three lateral passes before scoring a touchdown to bring the Saints to within a point of the Jags. It was an amazing play, but it was followed by one of the biggest anti-climaxes in NFL history when usually reliable kicker **John Carney** missed the extra point that would have tied the game. Despite the unlikely touchdown, the Saints were out of postseason contention.

THE PRO BOWL

★★★★★★★★★★★★★★★★★★★

The **Pro Bowl** has always been something of an anomaly on the NFL schedule. On one hand, it's an honour for a player to be picked as one of the best in his position. On the other hand, a Pro Bowl designation comes with an invitation to partake in a meaningless game in which everybody's primary aim is to avoid injury. To solve the conundrum, the Pro Bowl has recently been transformed into a combination of skills competitions and non-contact flag football games, a new format which lends itself to television and has makes the Pro Bowl a fun, low-intensity novelty for the lucky players who are invited.

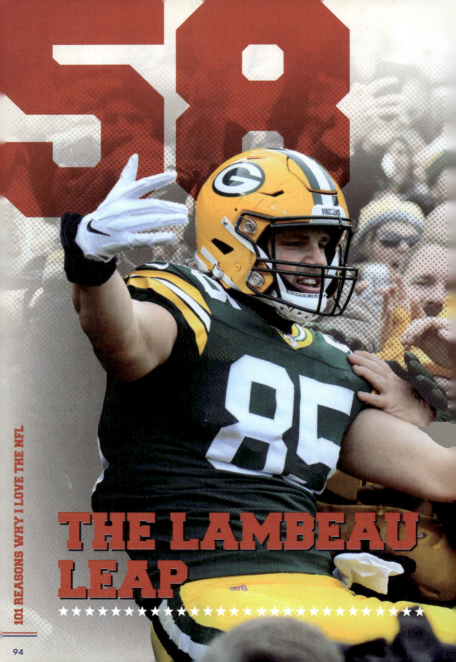

Green Bay Packers safety LeRoy Butler was ecstatic when he recovered a fumble and returned it to the Los Angeles Raiders end zone for his first NFL touchdown in 1993. He was so happy, in fact, that he leapt up the high wall separating spectators from the field of play and sat on top for a few moments while adoring Packers fans embraced him. It was the beginning of a new tradition at Lambeau Field. Ever since, Packers players have celebrated touchdowns with Green Bay's passionate fanbase, and the **Lambeau Leap** survived despite the NFL trying to crack down on elaborate touchdown celebrations in the 2000s.

Not every player has pulled off a Lambeau Leap successfully. Some failed to jump the required height (although the Packers have lowered the wall height since Butler's first leap) and others have had food and drink spilled on them. New York Giants running back Brandon Jacobs angered Packers fans by faking a Lambeau Leap during the 2007 NFC Championship Game, and Cincinnati Bengals wide receiver Chad Ochocinco planted some Bengals fans in the stands so he could perform the Packers' signature celebration. Given how iconic the Lambeau Leap has become, it's no surprise opposing players want to be part of the tradition.

59

THE GREATEST COMEBACK, PART 1

101 REASONS WHY I LOVE THE NFL

The New England Patriots were on familiar ground when they progressed to Super Bowl LI in February 2017. It was their eighth Super Bowl appearance since 2001, and they'd won four of them. The Atlanta Falcons, in contrast, had only one other Super Bowl appearance in franchise history, and were searching for their first title. But it was the Falcons who looked most comfortable when they started the game. They scored three second-quarter touchdowns to go 21-0 up and increased their led to 28-3 midway through the third quarter. The Patriots appeared down and out – but drew on their vast wealth of experience to claw back the deficit.

James White had two rushing touchdowns, Stephen Gostkowski kicked a field goal, and Danny Amendola caught the ball in the end zone. Tom Brady engineered two two-point conversions, and the Patriots tied the game with 57 seconds to go. The momentum was with the New England juggernaut going into overtime, and the tables inevitably turned when Brady led a 75-yard drive downfield. James White stretched over the line to score a walk-off Super Bowl-winning touchdown to cap the comeback of Super Bowl comebacks – no team had ever overturned a 25-point deficit in the season finale.

60

CANNON FIRE
★★★★★★★★★★★★

The Tampa Bay Buccaneers really embraced their nickname when they built Raymond James Stadium in 1998. Just beyond the seating area by the north end zone is a 100-metre-long replica **pirate ship**, complete with a selection of pyrotechnic cannons. The weapons fire a warning shot when the Bucs get into the red zone, and again in celebration of a Buccaneers scoring play (six shots for a touchdown, three for a field goal, one for an extra point). When the flags are lowered to reveal the Buccaneers logo, fans go wild in anticipation of another successful raid on an enemy franchise.

THE SALARY CAP

★★★★★★★★★★★★★★★★★★★★★★★★

The wealthiest NFL teams like the Dallas Cowboys and New England Patriots have billions of **dollars** on the balance sheet. If they ploughed their ample resources into signing the best free agents, the NFL would soon lose the parity it so values. To prevent inequality in roster expenditure, the salary cap limits the amount each team can spend on wages. The salary cap allows upwards of $200 million on salaries each year, but that's split between more than 50 players and the cap soon restricts spending if a team splashes the cash on a top quarterback, reliable offensive lineman or star receiver.

61

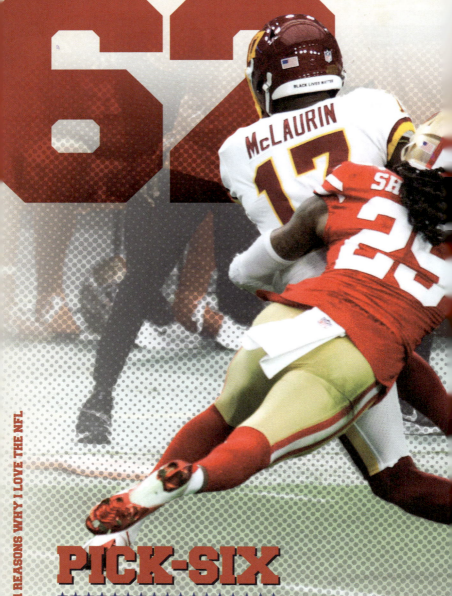

PICK-SIX

The job of a defensive back is to prevent a team making big yards on passing plays. Cornerbacks line up near the sidelines and safeties loiter in the middle, but both positions rely on their ability to track wide receivers and stop them catching the ball. A defensive back needs many of the same skills as the receivers they aim to stop: speed, agility and great hand-eye co-ordination. Among the greatest defensive backs to have patrolled the backfield in the NFL are Dick 'Night Train' Lane, who played for the Los Angeles Rams, Chicago Cardinals and Detroit Lions in the 1950s and 1960s, and Deion 'Prime Time' Sanders, who featured for several teams in the 1990s and early 2000s.

In more recent years, top cornerbacks and safeties have included **Richard Sherman**, Jalen Ramsey and Josh Norman. The best way for a defensive back to get recognition is to not just stop a receiver from catching the ball, but to catch it themselves. An interception immediately transfers possession, and it gives the intercepting player a chance to return the ball for a touchdown – or in NFL parlance, a pick-six. Rod Woodson is the all-time leader in pick-six interceptions with 12, his no-relation namesake Charles Woodson is next with 11.

THE PERFECT SEASON

Every season, when the last-remaining undefeated team loses its first game, the alumni of the 1972 Dolphins pop the champagne and toast the fact that their record has lasted another year – because the Dolphins of '72 are the only team to have gone through an entire regular season and postseason without losing. They amassed a 14-0 record in the regular season, then defeated the Browns, Steelers and Redskins to lift the Lombardi Trophy. Even more impressive is that they did most of it without starting quarterback **Bob Griese**, who broke his ankle in the week five matchup against the San Diego Chargers. But backup **Earl Morrall** stepped into the breach, ensuring that the Dolphins beat the Chargers 24-10, before guiding his team to victory after victory.

Morrall was harshly benched in the AFC Championship game and Griese returned to quarterback his team as they won the Super Bowl 14-7. The 1972 Dolphins had a relatively easy regular season schedule but, as the old adage says, you can only beat the team in front of you. The Dolphins did that with aplomb, leading the NFL in both points scored and fewest points allowed.

64

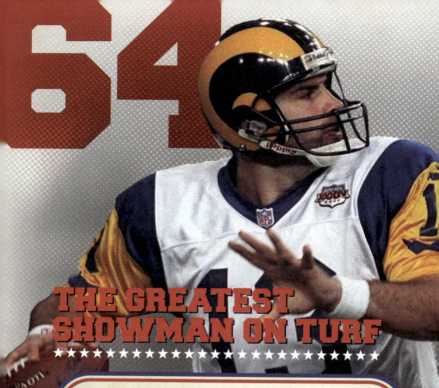

THE GREATEST SHOWMAN ON TURF

Kurt Warner took his time getting to the NFL. He wasn't chosen in the 1994 draft, nor did a team sign him as an undrafted free agent. He had little choice but to stack shelves at a supermarket before playing for the Iowa Barnstormers in the Arena Football League and Amsterdam Admirals in NFL Europe. Only in 1998 did the St Louis Rams sign Warner to their roster as a backup quarterback. But Warner got his chance in 1999 when starter Trent Green went down injured, and he led a high-powered offense nicknamed The Greatest Show on Turf to a Super Bowl win.

GUT-BUSTING LINEMEN

★★★★★★★★★★★★★★★★★★★★

Football is a game for all shapes and sizes. The fleet of foot are receivers and defensive backs. Power runners are running backs and linebackers. And those who don't really run at all? They're the **linemen**. These guys have chests and torsos that threaten to rip through their jerseys even before they put on their pads. Offensive linemen guard their quarterback or rusher by stopping a tackler pushing through the line of scrimmage, defensive linemen try to blast through to make a sack or tackle. Underestimate these big guys at your peril – a strong line is a vital part of a team's success.

68

TEAM NAMES

★★★★★★★★★★★★★★★

101 REASONS WHY I LOVE THE NFL

Like most other American team sports, NFL teams adopted nicknames early on. The first NFL season featured the Buffalo All-Americans and Canton Bulldogs among others. Since then, dozens of teams have come and gone, but one team name survives from the first days – the Chicago Cardinals are the same franchise that now bear that name in Arizona. Some names have fallen out of fashion. The **Washington Redskins** were criticised for years for a name that offended many. They were renamed the Commanders in 2022. Other names in the mix were Armada, Presidents, Redhawks, or the simple name they carried during the renaming process: Washington Football Team.

Other teams have switched names too. The New York Jets were once the Titans, the Pittsburgh Steelers were the Pirates, and the Chicago Bears were temporarily the Staleys. Other teams nearly chose alternative names when they were formed. The Dallas Cowboys' first owner initially pushed for the Dallas Rangers. A fan poll to name an expansion team in Baltimore also considered the Americans and Marauders before the Ravens won the vote. When the Houston Texans joined the league, owner Bob McNair picked from a shortlist of five that also included the Apollos, Bobcats, Stallions and Wildcatters.

67

101 REASONS WHY I LOVE THE NFL

AL MICHAELS

★★★★★★★★★★★★★★★★★★★★★★★

In the 1971 NFL Draft, the Boston Patriots had the first pick, and later that year they changed their name to the New England Patriots. The second pick was Archie Manning, father of future Super Bowl-winning quarterbacks Peyton and Eli. Though it seems a lifetime ago, 1971 also marked the NFL debut of sports broadcaster **Al Michaels**, who called his first game for NBC. More than 50 years later, he's still commentating. Michaels is known for broadcasting when several momentous sporting events took place: the Miracle on Ice at the 1980 Winter Olympics and the earthquake-interrupted game in baseball's 1989 World Series.

But it was during a 20-year stint as the lead play announcer on *Monday Night Football* that Michaels became a familiar voice in American households. He switched to *Sunday Night Football* when he moved networks, and he can still be heard on Amazon Prime's coverage of *Thursday Night Football*. Thanks to his conversant style and decades of experience in the broadcast booth, Michaels is the best-loved commentator in American sports, and many consider his easy rapport with John Madden on *Monday Night Football* to be the high-water mark in sports broadcasting.

68

MIRACLE AT THE MEADOWLANDS

★★★★★★★★★★★★★★★★★★★★★★★

There's no love lost between the **Philadelphia Eagles** and New York Giants, so Giants fans were already celebrating as their team ran out the clock against their rivals in 1978. All the Giants needed to do was protect the ball, and the Eagles were powerless to stop them since they had no timeouts left. But everything changed when quarterback Joe Pisarcik botched a handoff to Larry Csonka and the ball ended up on the floor. Eagles cornerback Herman Edwards snatched up the ball and ran it in for a fumble recovery touchdown to give the Eagles an unlikely victory.

101 REASONS WHY I LOVE THE NFL

JAW-DROPPING CATCHES

★★★★★★★★★★★★★★★★★★★

Wide receivers need to sprint from the line of scrimmage on a predetermined route and turn at the exact moment the ball flies to catch it – but they must do it with a defensive back breathing down their neck. Sometimes, it all comes together and results in a perfectly timed catch to push a team downfield. In recent years, receivers have made some spectacular catches in traffic, such as **Justin Jefferson's** falling-backwards grab to pluck the ball from a cornerback's hands and rescue the Minnesota Vikings on fourth-and-18 in 2022, or Odell Beckham Jr's one-handed catch in the end zone for the New York Giants in 2014.

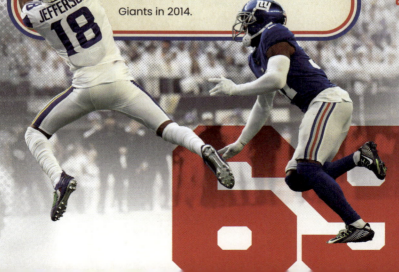

70

101 REASONS WHY I LOVE THE NFL

FREE AGENCY

When the Super Bowl is over and the offseason begins, all eyes turn towards the draft as teams look to rebuild for the future. When the draft is done, the offseason moves into a new phase: free agency. At this point, draft picks who've served their initial four- or five-year contracts can choose whether to sign with a new team or stay where they are. Of course, they need an offer on the table. After their first contract expires, veterans naturally expect a pay increase – and if a player is only just on the cusp of the roster, management may let them go and draft a younger, cheaper replacement.

But established stars who've proven themselves in the NFL will often benefit from a huge jump in wages, like Kansas City Chiefs quarterback **Patrick Mahomes**. He was paid $16.4 million over his first four years, but in year five, he signed a new deal with an enormous pay rise: $477 million over ten years. Mahomes stayed with the same team, but many free agents move to new pastures. Brett Favre, Deion Sanders and Reggie White all hit the headlines when they opted for unexpected new starts during free agency.

71

THE SHERIFF

★★★★★★★★★★★★★★★★★★★★

101 REASONS WHY I LOVE THE NFL

Peyton Manning was expected to be good: the son of a former NFL quarterback, a great college player, and the first overall pick by the Indianapolis Colts in 1998. He lived up to the lofty expectations. During the course of his first 14 years in Indiana, Manning never missed a game, was a four-time MVP and transformed the Colts into perennial championship contenders. He led his team to victory in Super Bowl XLI, and would probably have won more rings had it not been for the New England Patriots dominating the AFC.

Despite a five-year contract extension, Manning's tenure in Indianapolis came to a sudden end. He missed the entire 2011 season due to neck surgery and the Colts slumped to a 2-14 record without him. That gave them another number-one draft pick, and they used it to select Manning's successor, Andrew Luck. But Manning felt he had games left in the tank and, after the Colts released him, he signed with the Denver Broncos. It was a clever move. Manning's second season in Colorado saw him set all-time NFL records for passing yards and passing touchdowns, and he gained a second Super Bowl ring in his final season to retire from the sport as a champion.

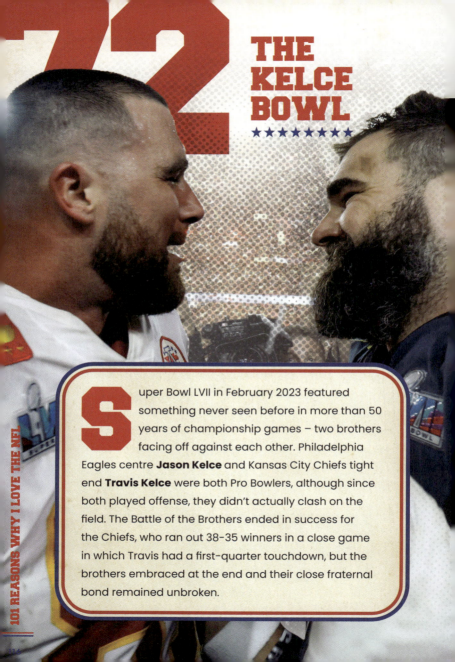

72

THE KELCE BOWL

Super Bowl LVII in February 2023 featured something never seen before in more than 50 years of championship games – two brothers facing off against each other. Philadelphia Eagles centre **Jason Kelce** and Kansas City Chiefs tight end **Travis Kelce** were both Pro Bowlers, although since both played offense, they didn't actually clash on the field. The Battle of the Brothers ended in success for the Chiefs, who ran out 38-35 winners in a close game in which Travis had a first-quarter touchdown, but the brothers embraced at the end and their close fraternal bond remained unbroken.

MVP

★★★★★★

Since 1938, a number of different organisations have tried to recognise the best player in each season with the Most Valuable Player award. Nowadays, the most prestigious MVP title is the Associated Press award, which has been given out since 1957. A panel of 50 sportswriters base their judgement on regular season performances, although the result isn't announced until Super Bowl Eve. According to the AP voters, the best player over the course of the past few decades is Peyton Manning, who was named MVP five times. **Aaron Rodgers** is a close second with four.

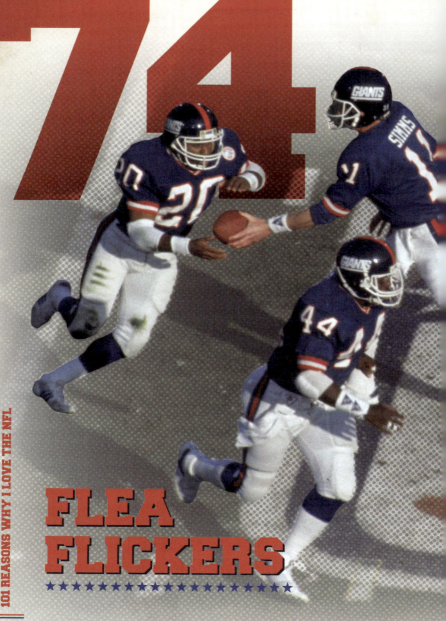

Most of the time, pass plays involve the quarterback flinging the ball downfield to a receiver in the hope of quickly gaining yards, but there are rules involved. Only one forward pass can be thrown, and it must be from behind the line of scrimmage. Passes can't go to a centre or guard, and only to a tackle if he declares himself eligible to the referee and other team. Laterals, on the other hand, can be thrown from anywhere on the field, to anyone, and by anyone.

There's just one caveat: the ball must go backwards. Quarterbacks regularly throw short laterals to a nearby running back to begin a rushing play, but most associate laterals with trick plays like the **flea flicker**. It was used to best effect by the New York Giants in Super Bowl XXI. Quarterback Phil Simms handed the ball to running back Joe Morris, but before Morris crossed the line of scrimmage, he lateralled the ball back to Simms, who launched a forward pass downfield for a 44-yard gain. If that's not special enough, there's another version of the flea flicker featuring multiple laterals before the ball returns to the quarterback.

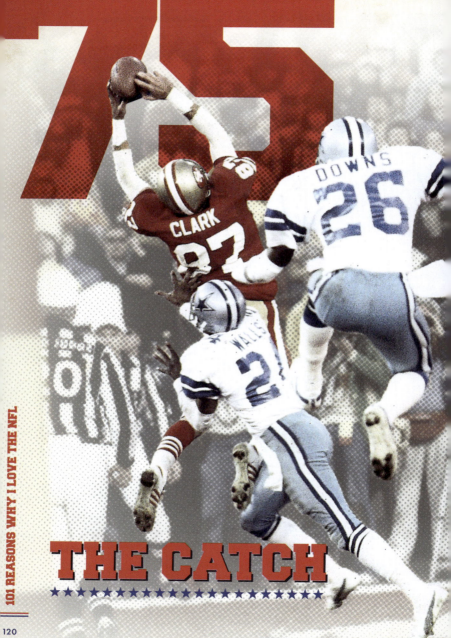

THE CATCH

The 1981 NFC Championship Game featured the conference's two best teams – the second-seed Dallas Cowboys at the top-seed San Francisco 49ers – and the game lived up to its billing. With one minute to go, the Cowboys had a slender six-point lead, but the 49ers were in the red zone and looking to score. On third-and-3 on the six-yard line, quarterback Joe Montana took a snap and backpedalled to his right. He intended to throw a quick pass to Freddie Solomon, just as he did on the exact same play earlier in the game. But this time, Solomon slipped. Montana waited for his other receivers to complete their routes, but no one managed to escape the secondary.

Montana continued to retreat, and the Cowboys sensed he was in trouble. Three defenders bore down on him for the sack, but at the last moment Montana spotted **Dwight Clark** had turned in the end zone and was running along the back boundary. Montana fired a pass, Clark caught it with his fingertips for a touchdown, and the 49ers took the lead on the extra point. The 49ers won the Super Bowl and The Catch came to signal the beginning of a new dynasty.

76

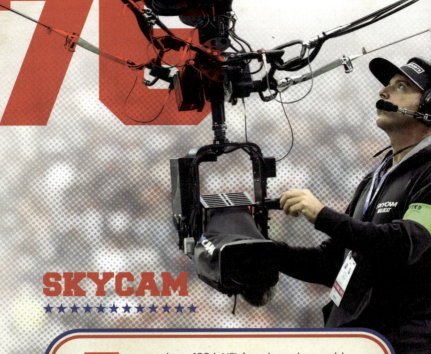

SKYCAM

★★★★★★★★★★★★★

As early as 1984, NFL fans have been able to feel part of the action as a television camera floats above the field. The remote-control camera shoots along four wires attached to each corner of the stadium and offers a bird's eye view of the action. It's a video-game style perspective that predates the *Madden NFL* video game franchise. **Skycam** has been a neat addition to the director's usual repertoire of shots, although one New England Patriots home game in 2017 was almost entirely broadcast from the Skycam after fog obscured the view from the normal sideline cameras.

MR IRRELEVANT

★★★★★★★★★★★★★★★★★★★★★★★★

It's the title every college player loves to hate. Mr Irrelevant is the name given to the final player selected in each year's draft – a moniker that reflects the fact that most players chosen that late are released before they get close to a team's active roster. That said, some Mr Irrelevants have bucked the trend. Marty Moore (1994), Jim Finn (1999) and **Ryan Succop** (2009) have won Super Bowl rings, while 2022 Mr Irrelevant Brock Purdy was cast into the San Francisco 49ers quarterback job following injuries to the starters and led his team to the NFC Championship in 2022 and 2023.

RAIDER NATION

The team now known as the Las Vegas Raiders have led a nomadic existence, but it was during their travels that a distinct identity was forged. As a near neighbour of San Francisco, Oaklanders revelled in their status as a no-nonsense, working-class community in comparison with the sleek yuppies of Silicon Valley, and the Oakland Raiders adopted the underdog attitude during the 1970s. The Raiders' brand was encouraged by their combative owner, Al Davis, the ginormous personality who ruled the franchise for its first 50 years.

When Davis relocated the Raiders to Los Angeles, they became the team of choice for the city's Black and Latino residents. Raider merchandise was regularly spotted in music videos thanks to prominent gangsta rappers like Cypress Hill and heavy metal bands like Metallica. Back in Oakland for a second stint, committed fans from Raider Nation created the Black Hole – a section of the Oakland Coliseum reserved for **fans dressed in elaborate and freaky costumes** using the black and silver colour scheme and skull motif. The Raiders are now based in Sin City, and its fans continue to demonstrate a level of devotion that few other teams can match.

Television cameras caught Minnesota Vikings cornerback Patrick Peterson offering his team an absurd challenge at half-time in their encounter with the Indianapolis Colts in December 2022: 'We need five touchdowns to win this game.' The Vikings were trailing 33–0, a margin no team had ever recovered from. That didn't stop the Vikings having a go. They scored a touchdown midway through the third quarter and again with a minute to go in the third. The Vikings then scored three times in the fourth quarter – all short passes by quarterback Kirk Cousins – to hit the five-touchdown target set by Peterson at half-time. A third-quarter Colts field goal meant that it wasn't enough to win the game, but it was enough to tie and send the game into overtime.

During a tense extra period, the Vikings turned down a long field goal opportunity and punted, but their defence stopped the Colts to give them another chance. This time, Cousins got his team into safer field goal range and kicker **Greg Joseph** converted it to cap the greatest comeback in NFL history. Colts quarterback Matt Ryan was on the wrong side of another embarrassing loss – Ryan was also quarterback when the Atlanta Falcons suffered the biggest Super Bowl comeback five years earlier.

80

THE TABLE SMASH

★★★★★★★★★★★★★★★★

In recent years, a new tradition has emerged at Buffalo Bills tailgates. Spectators gather around an excited fan who **throws themself onto a folding table**. If the table breaks, the watching tailgaters go bananas in celebration. Nobody quite knows why the odd pre-game ritual started, although it does bear resemblance to what happens on the field – perhaps a particularly brutal quarterback sack. The Bills franchise frowns upon the body-slamming of tables in its parking lots, but their supporters often ignore the rules – an appropriate response for a fanbase that likes to call itself The Mafia.

GATORADE SHOWER

★★★★★★★★★★★★★★★★

New York Giants tackle Jim Burt got a little carried away when he celebrated his team's victory over the Washington Redskins in October 1984. He'd endured a beasting from head coach Bill Parcells during practice the week before, so Burt picked up a cooler of iced Gatorade and dunked it over Parcells' head. It soon became a Giants tradition, and after John Madden marked up the Gatorade cooler on his telestrator in the 1986 playoffs, the **Gatorade shower** was adopted by other teams. Now, it's spread across all levels of all American sports and has even worked its way into Australian cricket and Brazilian soccer celebrations.

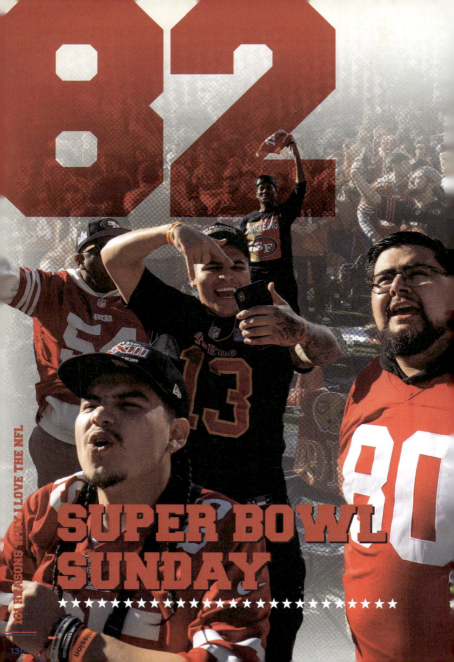

SUPER BOWL SUNDAY

Americans celebrate Thanksgiving on the fourth Thursday of November every year, but the second Sunday in February is almost as popular, despite not being an official public holiday. Since 2022, when the NFL calendar was extended by an extra week, the second Sunday marks the Super Bowl. Countless sports fans mark the date on their calendar and **gather with friends and family** to watch the big game. Even non-sports fans get in on the action, and thanks to these once-a-year viewers, the Super Bowl reliably records the year's highest television ratings. As Super Bowl Sunday has grown in scale over the years, Americans have learned to adapt their practices.

Stores expect lower footfall and give staff the day off. Churches move Sunday services so they don't clash with the game. Food delivery companies are twice as busy as usual. Water and energy companies expect lower demand during the game, but plan for a surge at half-time when fans rush to the toilet and heat up the coffee. Given the number of Super Bowl Sunday parties that take place, the American economy is less productive on the following Monday as hungover sports fans struggle to drag themselves into work.

SWEETNESS

unning back **Walter Payton** started his professional NFL career with the Chicago Bears in 1975 and remained at Soldier Field for 13 seasons. His teammates called him 'Sweetness' for his loveable personality, but on the field, Payton was a linebacker's nightmare. Payton broke records for the most career rushing yards, touchdowns, carries and yards from scrimmage. He had ten seasons with more than 1,000 yards, won the MVP award in 1977, helped the Bears win Super Bowl XX and was the league's rushing leader for five consecutive years from 1976 to 1980. Payton gained so many yards by playing to a style drilled into him by his college coach: never die easy.

Payton made the defence work for every tackle and rarely went out of bounds voluntarily. Payton faced a post-retirement battle with the same never-die-easy attitude. Twelve years after he hung up his boots, Payton was diagnosed with a rare liver disorder. Later that year, he died from complications that arose during his treatment. Shortly afterwards, the NFL announced that its Man of the Year Award – which Payton himself received in 1977 for his charitable endeavours – would now be known as the Walter Payton Man of the Year.

84

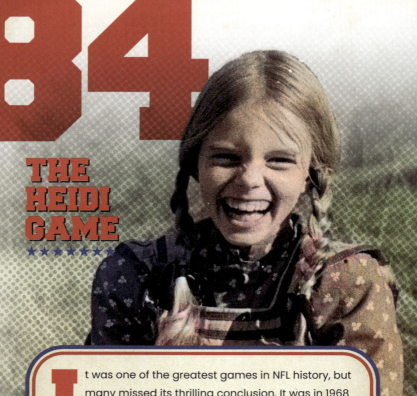

THE HEIDI GAME

★★★★★★★★

It was one of the greatest games in NFL history, but many missed its thrilling conclusion. It was in 1968 and with one minute to go, the New York Jets had outscored the Oakland Raiders 32-29, but thanks to injuries and penalties, the play clock was moving slowly. Thinking it was all over, bosses at NBC elected to end their coverage early and start broadcasting *Heidi* on time to avoid a delay to the schedule – but their decision meant millions of East Coast viewers missed out on the Raiders' thrilling two-touchdown comeback. Thanks to the predictable outcry from football fans, networks promised they wouldn't cut away in future.

101 REASONS WHY I LOVE THE NFL

ONSIDE KICKS

★★★★★★★★★★★★★★★★★★

Most of the time, kick-off tactics are simple – whack the ball as far as possible to pin the receiving team far back in its own territory. But near the end of a game, a losing team will often gamble with an **onside kick**. The ball is kicked short to give the kicking team a chance to get possession, and the kicker may deliberately cause the ball to bobble in the hope that the receiving team will fumble. The odds of success are slim, but onside kicks always provide entertainment as players dive to gain possession of the bouncing football.

THE HEIDI GAME - ONSIDE KICKS

86

THE HALF-TIME SHOW

101 REASONS WHY I LOVE THE NFL

The first few decades of the Super Bowl half-time were pretty tame and usually featured college marching bands parading around the field. By the 1990s, both the NFL and the television networks showing the game were keen to stop viewers channel-hopping at half-time, and asked Disney to make the half-time show more of an extravaganza. Their solution was a performance by hit boyband New Kids on the Block. In 1993, the NFL went all-out and hired the biggest star they could: Michael Jackson. Since then, the Super Bowl Half-Time Show has become a highlight of many performers' careers.

Acts are no longer paid a fee, but they can expect a huge surge in record sales and downloads, and the kudos of being a half-time headliner is vast. An entire stage is quickly erected during the slightly longer 30-minute interval, enabling singers to perform their greatest hits, often accompanied by equally famous backing artists and dozens of dancers. Among the superstars to take to the Super Bowl stage are Beyoncé, **Madonna**, The Rolling Stones and Prince – though none of their sets have been as famous as the revealing performance featuring Justin Timberlake and Janet Jackson at Super Bowl XXXVIII in 2004.

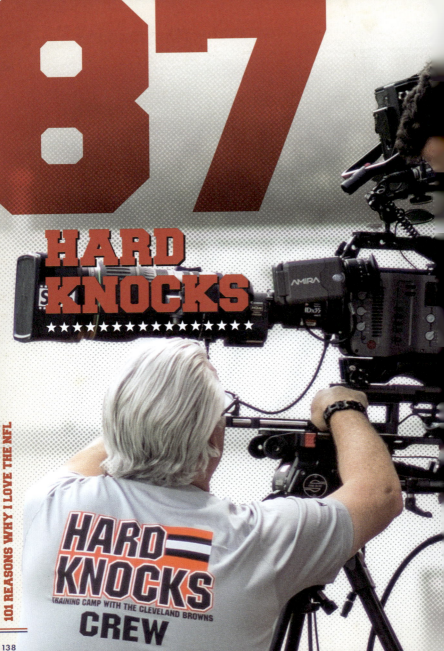

87
HARD KNOCKS

101 REASONS WHY I LOVE THE NFL

At the start of the 21st century, a new genre of television programming was beginning to hit the mainstream: reality TV. Thanks to smash hits like *Survivor* and *Big Brother*, viewers were getting used to watching warts-and-all footage of ordinary people. The NFL jumped on the bandwagon with ***Hard Knocks***, a behind-the-scenes documentary following one team's preseason preparations. Filming began with the reigning Super Bowl champion Baltimore Ravens in 2001 and Dallas Cowboys in 2002, and the Kansas City Chiefs featured in the series' 2007 reboot. Most teams dislike their dirty laundry being aired in public, so the NFL has set criteria that forces them to participate.

Teams are exempt from the program if they've participated in the previous ten years, have a new head coach, or have been in the playoffs in either of the previous two seasons – otherwise they're fair game for the cameras. Thanks to *Hard Knocks*, fans have been privileged to watch a Rex Ryan coaching meltdown in the New York Jets locker room, mighty nose tackle Vince Wilfork embrace the Texan lifestyle by going shirtless in dungarees, and the shock cut of Chad Ochocinco from the Miami Dolphins roster.

HARD KNOCKS

88

BILL BELICHICK'S RESIGNATION
★★★★★★★★★★★★★★★

On the day that **Bill Belichick** was supposed to be unveiled to the media as the new head coach of the New York Jets, he turned the press conference into a surprise resignation announcement. A few minutes earlier, he'd scrawled a famous note on a napkin: 'I resign as HC of the NYJ.' Belichick had received a better offer – head coach of the New England Patriots – and chose to dump the Jets. It was a defining moment in the history of both franchises. The Patriots went on to win six Super Bowls under Belichick, while the Jets slumped into two decades of mediocrity.

101 REASONS WHY I LOVE THE NFL

I'M GOING TO DISNEY WORLD!

★★★★★★★★★★★★★★★★★★★★★★

Sports broadcasters tend to ask the same predictable question when a player wins a championship: 'What are you going to do next?' **Disney** turned the trope into a marketing campaign, paying Super Bowl XXI MVP Phil Simms to record a commercial in which he was asked the usual question, and Simms replied, 'I'm going to Disney World!' Since then, Disney have recruited most Super Bowl MVPs to star in their own versions of the commercial, and the company invites the MVP to a special parade in their honour in the days after the big game.

There's some truth in the stereotype that Americans rarely travel abroad because they already have an entire world within its borders: from the beach to the mountains, there's every type of landscape. And with such diverse terrain comes huge variations in weather. NFL players must adapt to every type of weather conditions. Early season games in Florida, California and Texas almost break the thermometer. One 1971 match-up between the New Orleans Saints and Los Angeles Rams in New Orleans was played with a field temperature of 54 degrees Celsius. But come December, the Northern teams take the extreme in the other direction.

The famous Ice Bowl game in Green Bay was played in minus 26 degrees Celsius with a wind that made it seem even colder. There's also other extreme weather: a 1988 playoff game in Chicago was badly affected by fog, while the 1983 AFC Championship Game is known as the Mud Bowl for the torrential rain that fell in Miami. A statistical analysis in 2023 showed that the New England Patriots are the best performers in freezing conditions, but the top team in heatwave games was more of a surprise: the **Pittsburgh Steelers**.

91

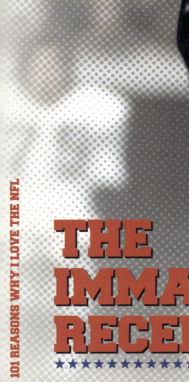

THE IMMACULATE RECEPTION

101 REASONS WHY I LOVE THE NFL

THE IMMACULATE RECEPTION

It seemed like the Pittsburgh Steelers had no chance. They trailed the Oakland Raiders 7-6 with 22 seconds to go in the divisional round of the 1972 playoffs. They were on fourth-and-10 on their own 40-yard line. The Steelers needed divine intervention – and they got it. Terry Bradshaw dropped back for a passing play, hoping to give his receivers time to blast upfield, but Bradshaw came under pressure and had to let the ball go earlier than intended. The ball flew over the line of scrimmage towards halfback John Fuqua, but Fuqua was tackled by Raiders safety Jack Tatum and the ball bounced free.

It fell into the hands of running back **Franco Harris**, who was supposed to be a blocker on the play. Harris set off downfield, evaded a tackle, benefited from a block, and stiff-armed a final tackler to score a touchdown. The Immaculate Reception, as the play has come to be known, is remembered as one of the greatest moments in the history of football – as well as one of the most controversial, as Raiders and Steelers fans still debate whether it was a legal play depending on whether Tatum touched the ball as he tackled.

92

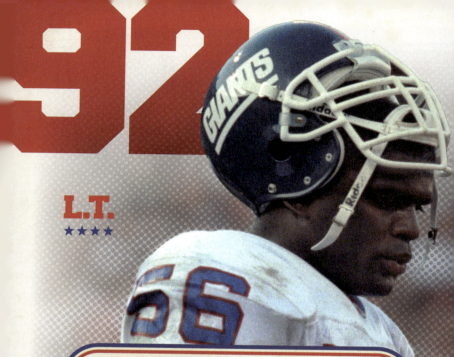

L.T.
★ ★ ★ ★

Probably the greatest defensive player of all time, **Lawrence Taylor** redefined the role of linebacker and gave offensive co-ordinators nightmares thanks to his ability to break through the offensive line and sack the quarterback. He demonstrated his combination of speed and strength to gruesome extent when Joe Theismann suffered a compound fracture during a Taylor tackle in 1985. The following year, Taylor was given the rare accolade of NFL MVP as a defensive player, and was a three-time Defensive Player of the Year. He ended his career with 133 sacks and had double-digit season sacks every year from 1984 to 1990.

SUPER BOWL RINGS

The Super Bowl winning team is presented with a trophy in recognition of their victory, but the players must wait for their official memento: a **bespoke ring**. The NFL contributes up to $7000 per item, any additional costs must be borne by the team. The extra expense is often substantial – the rings presented by the New England Patriots for winning Super Bowl XLIX reportedly cost $36,500 each. Exactly who gets a ring is the choice of the team: aside from players and coaches who took part in the postseason, teams may choose to include inactive and injured players, executives and backroom staff.

CELEB FANS

Basketball games often feature A-list celebs taking advantage of their fame to snag the best courtside seats. But many celebs love football too, and proudly wear their teams' colours. **Jon Bon Jovi** and Mark Wahlberg follow the New England Patriots. Both President Bushes are fans of the Houston Texans, Eminem can often be seen at Detroit Lions games, Samuel L. Jackson is an Atlanta Falcons fan, and George Clooney is all-in on the Cincinnati Bengals. Most Americans follow the team located nearest to where they were born, but NFL fans who were born abroad have a free choice and pick whichever team takes their fancy.

British actor Daniel Radcliffe enjoys watching the New York Giants, and it's fitting that England soccer player Harry Kane follows the New England team in the NFL. Some celeb fans put their money where their mouth is, like singer Marc Anthony, who has a minority stake in the Miami Dolphins. Others switch allegiances. Taylor Swift caused a sensation when she started dating Kansas City Chiefs tight end Travis Kelce and turned up to watch Super Bowl LVIII, cheering joyfully when the Chiefs won. The problem? Swift was supposed to be a die-hard fan of their opponents, the Philadelphia Eagles.

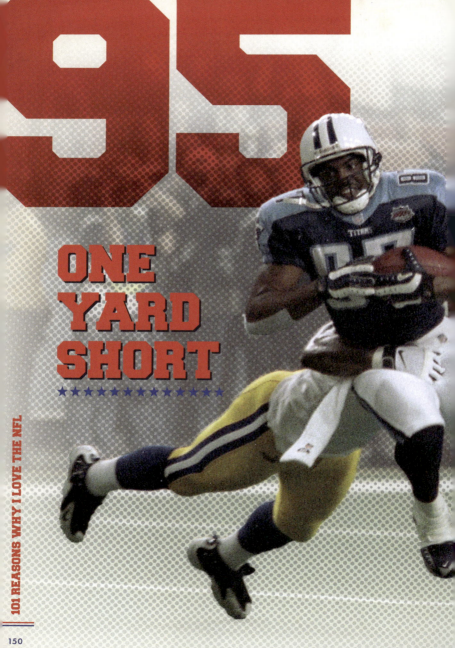

St Louis Rams head coach Dick Vermeil put together a hot offense in 1999 led by undrafted free agent quarterback Kurt Warner. The Greatest Show on Turf outscored their opponents 526-242 in the regular season en route to Super Bowl XXXIV, where they came up against the effective defence of the Tennessee Titans. The Super Bowl began with the Rams scoring 16 unanswered points, before the Titans clawed it back to 16-16. The Rams scored a touchdown with less than two minutes to go to take the lead again, only for the Titans to race downfield to the Rams' 10-yard line with one play to go.

If they scored, the game would surely go to overtime. The play seemed to go to plan. Receiver **Kevin Dyson** ran a central route and caught the ball five yards from the end zone, but linebacker **Mike Jones** appeared seemingly from nowhere. He wrapped his arms around Dyson's waist and the two players rolled to the floor with Dyson desperately reaching out to the end zone, but to no avail. Replays showed that he was inches short of a touchdown, and Jones had recorded the most clutch tackle in Super Bowl history.

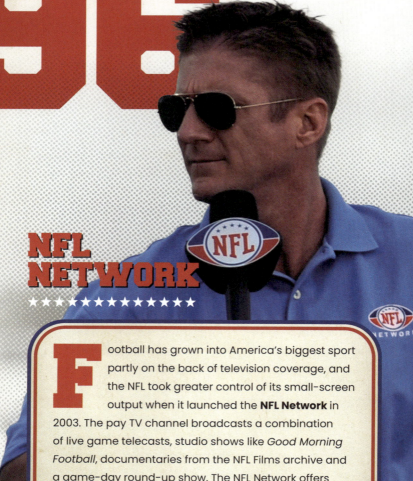

96

NFL NETWORK

★★★★★★★★★★★★

Football has grown into America's biggest sport partly on the back of television coverage, and the NFL took greater control of its small-screen output when it launched the **NFL Network** in 2003. The pay TV channel broadcasts a combination of live game telecasts, studio shows like *Good Morning Football*, documentaries from the NFL Films archive and a game-day round-up show. The NFL Network offers international fans an easy way to get their football fix without relying on the patchy coverage in their home country, and gives US fans a greater selection of games to choose from, including some college games.

101 REASONS WHY I LOVE THE NFL

HEAD PROTECTION

★★★★★★★★★★★★★★★★★★★★★★★★★

Nowadays, the helmet is probably the single most recognisable piece of NFL gear, but it wasn't always so. Although many players wore **leather** or cloth caps in the sport's early days, helmets were only made mandatory in 1943 thanks to rising safety concerns. At first, plastic and metal headgear was allowed. Now, helmet manufacturers use advanced materials and technology, and only a limited number of rigorously tested models are authorised for NFL games. As of 2024, players can also wear soft-shell guardian caps on top of their helmets as an extra layer of protection against life-changing concussions.

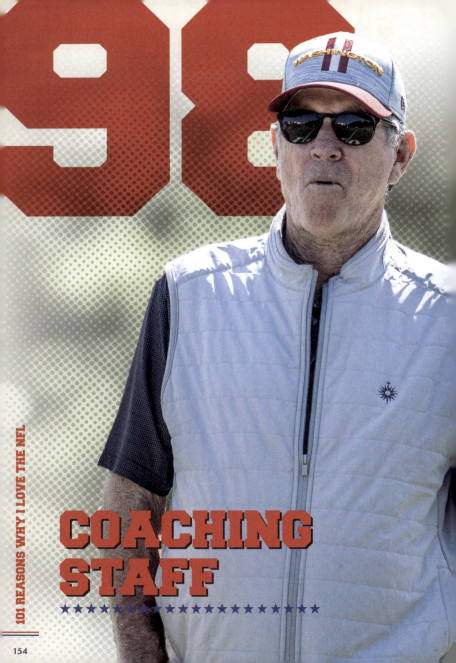

From monster lineman to speedy receivers, each player needs a specific set of skills, and teams employ various coaches who concentrate all their attention on a chosen speciality. There's a hierarchy to each team's coaching staff. Some coaches work only with a particular position group. Offensive and defensive coordinators run the entire offense and defence. They write the plays and call during games, while a third coordinator – the special teams coordinator – runs the show for punts, field goals and kick-offs. Coordinators are the step below the head coach, who must decide the team's overall strategy and style of play, and most new head coaches are recruited from within the NFL's cohort of coordinators.

However, many coordinators are unsuited to the top job and produce their best work as an underling. **Norv Turner** was an elite offensive coordinator for eight different NFL teams and won two Super Bowl rings with the Dallas Cowboys, but didn't enjoy the same degree of success as head coach of the Washington Redskins and Oakland Raiders. Similarly, Josh McDaniels was a key part of the New England Patriots dynasty of Tom Brady and Bill Belichick, but failed as head coach of the Denver Broncos and Las Vegas Raiders.

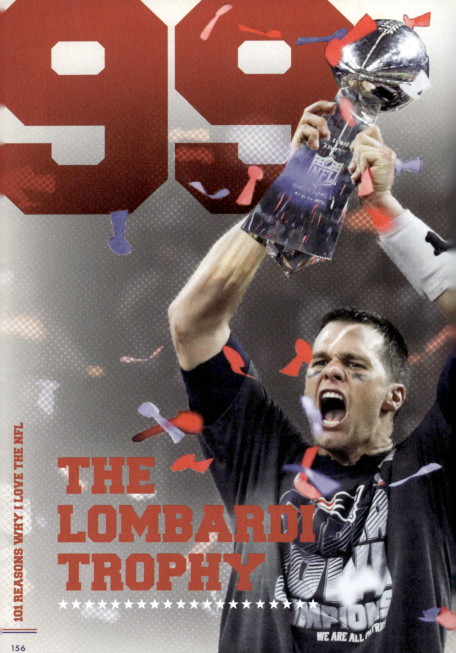

When the bosses of the NFL came together to plan the first World Championship Game in 1967 – what would later be designated the first Super Bowl – they decided to create an iconic trophy. The responsibility fell to Tiffany's vice-president Oscar Riedner, who decided on a football positioned on a three-sided concave stand. In 1970, three months after being diagnosed with colon cancer, Vince Lombardi died. Under Lombardi's leadership, the Green Bay Packers had won the first two Super Bowls, and the NFL soon decided to rename the championship trophy in his honour.

The new **Lombardi Trophy** was first awarded to the Baltimore Colts after they returned to their locker room after winning Super Bowl V in 1971. Only in 1996, when the Dallas Cowboys won Super Bowl XXX, was the trophy presented in a ceremony on the field. Each Super Bowl features a brand-new version of the Lombardi Trophy for the winning team to keep in perpetuity, and the only team that doesn't still have theirs is the Indianapolis Colts – the 1970 trophy they won as the Baltimore Colts remains in Baltimore as part of the legal settlement that followed their midnight flit in 1984.

100

THE BUTT FUMBLE

★★★★★★★★★★★★★

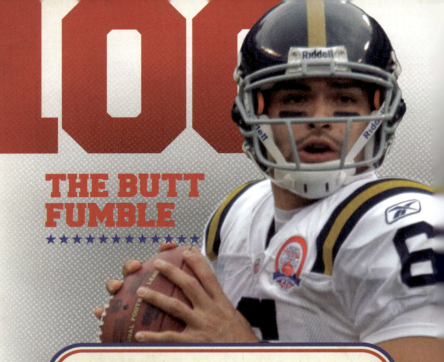

When journeyman quarterback **Mark Sanchez** tried to run with the ball during his fourth season with the New York Jets in 2012, he lowered his head for the charge – but his helmet collided with the backside of his own offensive lineman and Sanchez fumbled the ball. To add even more anguish, it was against the Jets' biggest rivals – the New England Patriots – and the Patriots returned the ball for a touchdown. The bum play was immediately named the Butt Fumble and went down in history as one of the NFL's most comical moments, although Sanchez probably doesn't see it that way.

TERRIBLE TOWELS

As fan traditions go, the Pittsburgh Steelers have an odd one – waving a bright yellow towel in the air. It started with radio analyst Myron Cope, who waved a towel from his position in the broadcast booth in 1975 to inspire the home support at Three Rivers Stadium. Forty years on, thousands of Steelers fans still wave their **Terrible Towels** in the air, making for a memorable sight. Profits from the sale of official towels are donated to charity, while committed Steelers fans have carried their towels to the top of Mount Everest and into space aboard the International Space Station.

About the Author

Scott Reeves is an award-winning sportswriter who has authored seven books and contributed to several guides to the NBA, NFL and college football.

He lives in Shropshire and is an avid follower of the Boston Celtics and NewEngland Patriots.

Photography courtesy of

Getty images, Alamy and Wiki Commons

Photographs: All copyrights and trademarks are recognised and respected